Afghanistan:

The Eye of a Storm

Afghanistan:

The Eye of a Storm

David Potts

ISBN: 979-8-738-44282-7

For Sam, Luke, and Mariette

CONTENTS

Introduction

Just before I went to Afghanistan, a friend and mentor cheerfully told me that wars there traditionally have three phases. *"In Phase One foreign forces invade, quickly capture Kabul, and set up a compliant Afghan regime. In Phase Two everything goes wonderfully well, especially in Kabul, but the foreigners and the central government fail to control the countryside. In Phase Three it all goes wrong, and everyone gets killed".* I was there in Phase Two.

This is my story based on a journal and notes jotted down in the first half of 2005. It places me at the centre of my world like a small child with limited horizons. The narrative is a fragment of what went on, so apologies for the many omissions and any inaccuracies. I produce it now because my three children, then aged six and under, have expressed an interest. It is intended to be enjoyed by them and others with sparse knowledge of military matters or Afghanistan. It is also another testimonial for the historical record of those who served there.

My job was to oversee Provincial Reconstruction Teams or PRTs as they were called. These were small outposts located in key provincial centres across much of Afghanistan. My visits to them are the backbone of this story.

The idea of PRTs was to extend the influence of central government into the provinces. This was supposed to be through local 'Security Sector Reform.' That meant helping Provincial Governors exercise their authority; promoting capable and accepted policing; delivering security sector infrastructure such as police stations or court houses; and helping mediate local conflict resolution between competing factions.

It was hoped their presence would help create a climate for aid agencies and others to conduct post conflict reconstruction and development activities such as delivering wells, medical care, schools, and roads.

Many aid agencies were wary of PRTs. They felt being associated with them exposed them to security risks or might inhibit local cooperation. Some objected in principle to military involvement in reconstruction activities.

I was in the United Nations mandated International Security Assistance Force (ISAF). It was there to help the Government of the Islamic Republic of Afghanistan stabilize the country. The Afghans had requested such a force. The North Atlantic Treaty Organization (NATO) of primarily the US, Canada, Turkey, and the Europeans provided it.

How it worked in Afghanistan was that individual NATO member nations agreed to take on responsibility for providing troops in specific geographic areas, such as a province or a city, or to deliver key military capabilities to support ISAF, such as helicopters or transport aircraft.

In practice, the forces deployed into Afghanistan, including in PRTs, reported to their own national military command structures back in their home countries. This limited ISAF's authority. Nations also applied 'caveats' to the use of their forces – "they can do this but not that, go here but not there", which added gravel to ISAF's gearbox.

Bigger nations took turns to provide the leadership and core elements of the headquarters in

Kabul that directed and managed ISAF on a day-to-day basis. When I was there Turkey provided the headquarters.

I also had a remit to lead ISAF's interactions with those delivering Counter Narcotics, Afghan National Police development and Justice Reform. These were three of five 'Security Reform' strands led by the G8 (Group of eight countries - the world's seven largest developed economies, plus Russia). I also led work within the headquarters on ISAF's input to 'Disarming Illegal Armed Groups' – which is what it says on the tin.

Afghanistan sits at a great Eurasian crossroads. Throughout its long history, this mixed blessing brought trade, wealth, religious and cultural influences, influxes of peoples and periodic destructive invasions. It lay between the Russian Empire and British India (which included Pakistan); between Persia (now Iran) and Arabia in the Southwest, and the great riches of China and India; and between the civilizations of India and Persia, and the nomads from the vast steppes of Central Asia and Mongolia.

Geography matters in Afghanistan. Travel is limited by snow and ice in the freezing winters and by sandstorms in the scorching summers. The Duke of Wellington, of Waterloo fame, once described it as a land of *"rocks, sands, desert, ice and snow"*.

Basically, the Hindu Kush, part of the Western Himalayas, flows across Afghanistan from Northeast to West. This inhospitable expanse of rock and mountain straddles the country, covering about 60% of it. Some of its peaks are over 20,000 feet (6,000 meters).

Southwest of the mountains is desert. North of them is steppe-like up to the Amu Darya river, which forms much of Afghanistan's northern border. It is about the size of Germany and Switzerland plus the Benelux countries and Denmark, or Texas if you are an American.

The population in 2005 was an estimated 26 million with five main ethnicities and many less numerous ones. Pashtuns (sometimes called Pathans) are the largest ethnic group but not a majority. Their heartland is in the East and South, and over in North-West Pakistan, but large numbers live in many other parts of the country. Turkmen live in the West and Northwest and in Turkmenistan. Uzbeks live in the North and in Uzbekistan, and Tajiks in the Northeast and Tajikistan. The Hazaras in the centre and West are a Mongolic people. Smaller ethnic groups include Baloch in the Southwest and in Pakistan and Iran, and various nomadic peoples.

All these ethnicities mix in the major cities, especially Kabul and the cities of the North and West. The major ethnicities are Sunni Moslems, except the Hazara who are Shi'ites.

Many languages are spoken in Afghanistan. Principally, Pashtu, mother tongue of the Pashtuns, and Dari, a form of Persian spoken by the Tajiks. Quite a simplification and both are widely spoken.

Afghanistan is in a tough neighbourhood surrounded by Pakistan, Iran, three 'Stans' of the former Soviet Union – Turkmenistan, Uzbekistan, and Tajikistan - and just touches China. It has been invaded many times over centuries, indeed millennia.

The 1979 Soviet invasion plunged Afghanistan into a decades-long Game of Thrones-like Dark Ages, with modern weaponry and religious fanaticism layered over. The Taliban took over a few years after the Soviets left. Their viciously oppressive fundamentalist regime and continuing warfare reduced the already devastated country to a dystopian wasteland. The 9/11 attacks by Al Qaeda, then holed-up in Afghanistan, triggered the US-led invasion and subsequent stabilization and reconstruction efforts. This 'Terrible Recent History' is summarized at the back.

We were not there to remake Afghanistan as a sort of Switzerland, just to provide its long-suffering people with the prospect of some modest prosperity and sufficient stability and security to stop the Taliban and Al Qaeda from coming back.

Being there seemed purposeful.

Week One
(Kabul and Maimana)

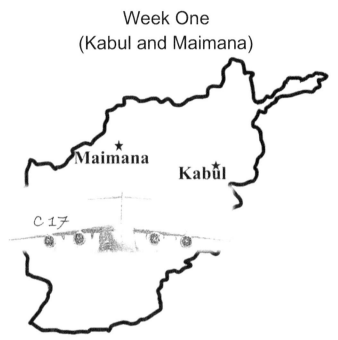

Saturday

Arrive in Kabul off a Jumbo-sized C17 Globemaster military jet that the UK has leased from the US. Its cargo is a lorry, pallets of stores and about 50 passengers. I slept on top of my sleeping bag in the cavernous cargo area.

Bright sunshine in Kabul but icy cold – snow everywhere. A curtain of jagged snowy mountains surrounds the city. I am driven in a white Nissan Patrol to the nearby UK base at 'Camp Souter': former warehouses of some sort. Straight into a series of briefings in a large shed. Corporal giving the medical briefing tells us the air in Kabul has the highest faecal matter content of any city on earth. I ask, *"What is the medical advice?"* and he says, *"Don't breathe sir."*

Evening: walk round camp with the Quartermaster. Freezing cold. I am chilled right through to my marrow. Helicopter approaches in the darkness, fires its defensive flares and zigzags away. Supper in Camp Souter with Nick Pound, a Royal Marine I am to take over from and Robert Mills, a Guards Lieutenant Colonel who would work directly for me. He proves a trusted friend and immense help.

Sunday

For now, I am to live with the Brits in Camp Souter. I have a single room with a bunk and a lockable wardrobe. Ablutions are down a corridor. The place is an ice box. I have assorted combat gear for work and play, sports kit for fitness training, and a pair of deck shoes. I have a pistol slung on my hip most of the time. A flak jacket is worn outside secure areas and a helmet kept to hand.

Nick's driver and protection team that I will inherit show up. They are a bunch of chipper infantry guys from the Wooster and Sherwood Foresters (Woofers). They drive me through Kabul in the Nissan Patrol to the NATO/ISAF compound where I will eventually be based.

Eurocorps, a Franco-German led outfit normally based in Strasbourg, currently provides the ISAF headquarters. It will soon move out freeing up space for the Turkish headquarters that I am to be part of.

Morning of discussions with Nick and a walk about in the ISAF camp. Quite a large walled-in area. The PRT office is in the substantial two-storey headquarters building that houses offices and briefing rooms. Its exterior is rendered in yellow ochre and it has a grey slate roof. Outside it, a few flags hang limply from overly tall flagpoles.

Most of the camp is just rows and rows of white 'Corimec' shelter accommodation, basically twenty-foot containers clipped together and popped on top of each other to form a two-storey structure.

Corimecs at ISAF Headquarters

There is a canteen where everyone eats three meals a day; latrines; a gym and a couple of small shops selling cold drinks, snacks, cigarettes, and Afghan nick-nacks. There is a bar somewhere too.

Afternoon: go on patrol with a UK team from Camp Souter. We begin with a formal set of orders setting out where we are going and actions to take on this or that happening. Threats we are briefed on include sticky bombs being placed on the side of the vehicle, suicide bombers with explosive vests, and a machine gun shoot with a heavy weapon. It all sounds a bit dramatic.

We travel in two black Toyota Land Cruisers, as conspicuous as anything could be, and are heavily armed – at least the team are – I have my standard issue L9A1 Browning 9mm Pistol. My pre-deployment training had included a test on it, which to my astonishment I passed with flying colours. I also had to run round the block, do a few push-ups, and bit of First Aid. That was it. I am not complaining: any more would have exceeded my attention span.

Kabul reminds me of Jaipur or Udaipur in Rajasthan, India, which I visited a few years ago. Busy slow traffic of beaten-up cars, lorries and small motorbikes interspersed with bony horses and donkeys amid a teeming mass of people.

The Afghans have lived-in faces. They seem a bit stern. Maybe from seeing us, but more likely on account of it being biting cold.

Most of the men are in drab modern garb. Some wear traditional 'shalwar kameez' of baggy trousers and long shirts that flow beneath their winter coats. Many are bare headed, but most sport some form of headdress.

Some are in scruffy turbans that to the untutored eye seem made from long checkered dish cloths. Pakols are popular, aka Chitrali caps - traditional Afghan flat topped, round hats of thick wool cloth, usually in sombre colours. Little white Topi or Kufi caps are common too and can be used as a core around which to wrap a turban, they can also be in brightly coloured patterns. The quintessential Karakul sheepskin hat, a sort of mini-Astrakhan often worn by President Karzai, is likely quite expensive and is rarely seen. But the star prize for the most common headdress goes to the knitted woollen Benny Hat that we would all recognize.

Women are similarly drab, mostly with headscarves of varying styles. Many, about a third or so, are shrouded head to floor in blue burqas, also known as chadaree. These have no slits for the eyes, as would be the case in a niqab, the woman within is required to peer through a gauze, eliminating her peripheral vision. The burqa denies her any public identity.

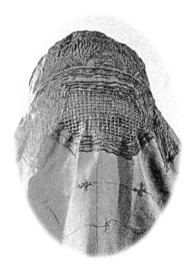

Traffic crawls along. There are a few crowded blue and white buses, lots of yellow Toyota Corolla taxis and a mixture of scruffy lorries. Huge, very brightly painted 'Jingle Trucks', that come up from Pakistan, lumber by laden with all manner of scrap and produce. An open sided flat-bed lorry crosses our view with twenty or more burqa clad women sitting on it like cargo, some with children on their laps. Streets are lined with hawkers and vendors selling anything and everything. Here and there men pull heavily laden handcarts, as if they were beasts of burden. Pedestrians shuffle along on the sidewalk and in the road, some jabbering on mobile phones.

We are quickly locked-in by the slow traffic and surrounded by the bustle of people who push past our vehicles, pockets full of those 'sticky bombs' no doubt.

"Immersion", the team call it.

Monday

Embarked on my recce of the Provincial Reconstruction Teams (PRTs). Basically, a NATO nation agrees to lead a PRT and then other, usually smaller nations, agree to contribute to it.

Plan is to fly to Maimana PRT, which is UK-led, for two days and then spend about a day or so each in Mazar-e-Sharif (UK), Konduz and Faisabad (Germany), and Pol-e Khumri (the Netherlands).

Nick would remain in Kabul throughout, but Robert and my team will fly up with our vehicles to join me at some point. We will drive back to Kabul over the Hindu Kush via the Salang Tunnel. Turns out Robert is determined to drive through the Salang Tunnel during his time in Afghanistan and takes every opportunity to plan on doing so. The Salang Tunnel had been built by the Russians in 1964 as a friendly neighbour project. It was a feat of engineering at the time and is now the main routeway through the Hindu Kush connecting Kabul to the North of the country – and indeed Pakistan to Central Asia.

Fly to Maimana on a Portuguese C130 Hercules, the standard military workhorse for short haul air movement of troops and logistics. It can land on dirt strips and has four propellors and a tail ramp.

C130

I sit up on the flight deck on a short bench seat behind the pilots. Maimana is close to the border with Turkmenistan and on the fringes of the infinite steppe of

Central Asia. Terrain on approach looks like endless desert.

Land on a dirt strip runway in bright sunshine. Hot, which is a shock after Kabul. The town is of basic mudbrick low-rise buildings. The mudbricks are sundried, rather than kiln fired, clay is applied over by hand. Roofs are flat and made by laying poles then layers of straw and mud. Interspersed are some more-recent, low-rise concrete structures also with flat roofs. Most are situated within walled enclosures of traditional mudbrick or concrete. Seriously drab. Local people here are largely Turkic or Uzbek and look like the descendants of the horsemen who roamed the Central Asian steppes, which is exactly what they are.

Although entirely unplanned, I am in time for a 'reception' in honour of the opening of a local radio station funded by USAID and Canada. Canadian Ambassador, USAID reps, UN local staff and the Provincial Governor of Faryab province (Abdul Latif) attend. Reception consists of sandwiches, cans of coke, and coffee and is served in the PRT's austere briefing room. Abdul the governor is an Uzbek with a dark overcoat and tie. His mobile goes off at regular intervals and he moves to the side to take the calls. All the guests leave Maimana immediately after the reception.

Rest of afternoon is spent on briefings by the UK, Norwegian and Finnish crew, and orientation to the small PRT. It's located in a former bank inside a walled compound, secure relative to other buildings in the town.

Maimana PRT

The PRT was originally all British, but the plan is to pass it over to the Nordic nations. There are still twenty to thirty Brits about and now twenty or so each of Finns and Norwegians. They are mostly military but with a small civilian component of Foreign Affairs, Development ministry, and Police representatives. The Brit Commander is away at present.

The PRT focusses on 'Security Sector Reform'. Here that is essentially about getting the police up and running and promoting a positive relationship between the Provincial Governor, Police, and the people. Its presence also provides a comfort blanket for all manner of civilian aid agencies to operate.

Evening meal at 1800 hours after which we have a briefing and prepare for the patrol I am to go on the next day. Patrolling is the bedrock of much military activity and generally involves small lightly equipped teams, sometimes roving over quite great distances. Their form and nature vary with the security environment. Faryab, the province we are in, is relatively benign.

Patrols can show a reassuring presence or gather information on natural disasters, security incidents, local security capabilities or malign actors etc. In hostile communities, people might face retribution if seen talking with a patrol. A fleeting presence can be easily replaced by nefarious forces once the patrol has moved on. So good patrolling is a challenge.

Earlier in my military life, I enjoyed patrolling in Northern Ireland as good military craic (Irish/Scots: lively, enjoyable, sociable), despite the ever-present threat of being shot at or blown up or whatever and the need to be constantly alert. In truth I always harboured a nagging doubt as to whether patrol activity there achieved what we imagined.

In patrolling, as with all else, *"The best laid schemes o' mice an' men gang aft agley" (or go awry)* as Robbie Burns puts it. One rain swept night, RAF Puma helicopters unintentionally dropped me and my patrol just inside the Republic of Ireland. Lights came on in nearby farmhouses and dogs barked their heads off in the mad way Irish dogs do. We scurried back across the border and had a good laugh about it all, and again later back in camp over the permitted 'Two Cans' of beer. Great craic.

Anyway, the purpose of the patrol tomorrow is just to give me a feel for the area and what it is like to go on a patrol here; should be fun. I sleep in the sick bay where there are two metal cots – the only bed spaces available in the PRT.

Tuesday
0700 breakfast of herrings and eggs, although an English fry-up was available.

0900 I set off with Mobile Observation Team (MOT) Kilo who are all Norwegian. Kasper is the patrol leader and Jan, the PRT Deputy Commander, comes for the ride. They are well armed, and we travel in two white Toyota Land Cruisers.

The plan is to do a slow loop of about a hundred kilometers following a track on a southerly circuit to bypass the town of Almar and then approach it from the west. We would then continue home northwards, and then eastwards, on another dirt road.

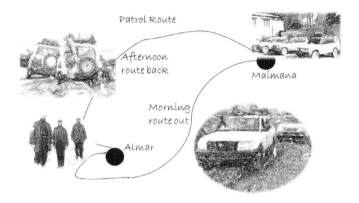

We travel west of Maimana on a dirt road and then turn south onto the track. The Norwegians play pop music from their iPods over the car stereo system. This amuses and makes me feel a bit like Captain Willard in *Apocalypse Now*, heading up the Nung River in Chief's patrol boat with the crew blasting out the Rolling Stones.

The landscape looks like desert with rolling dunes a few hundred feet high. On closer inspection, every inch of land has been brought under the plough. Dots on the hillside turn out to be men or boys ploughing, sometimes with pairs of small oxen pulling makeshift wooden ploughs with a single digging shaft that cuts one furrow at a time. There are herds of small goats everywhere tended by boys or by men with handsome Kuchi dogs (Afghan Shepherd dogs). They look nothing like an Afghan hound, much more like those Japanese Akita, or a Husky.

17

The villages are entirely of single storey buildings in mudbrick, each in a small compound of mudbrick walls. They teem with children and the odd woman shuffles about in a burqa. Everyone disappears indoors at the sight of us. It's as if we've ridden into an adobe village in a 'Spaghetti Western', like Agua Caliente in *For A Few Dollars More*. As the bandits approach it, their leader El Indio turns to Manco, the Clint Eastwood character, and growls, *"It looks like a morgue and could so easily be one"*.

There are a few camels about – Bactrian camels, great double humped hairy things. Traffic around and between the villages is mainly by donkey – lots of individuals and small groups moving about on donkeys, often with heavy or impossibly large loads on the animals.

A common sight is a man on foot leading a donkey with a woman in a burqa on its back. Just like the Biblical Joseph and Mary 2,000 years ago. I feel slightly cheated. Their arrival in Bethlehem by donkey seemed exceptional in childhood when told in 'Sunday School'. It was clearly as mundane then as arriving somewhere nowadays in a small family car.

There are quite a few little motorbikes about too. We dismount and chat to a couple of likely lads who are whizzing along on one.

We pull-up on a hillside to snack from our

packed lunches of sandwiches, fruit, cold boiled eggs, chocolate bars, crisps and cans of pop. I chat with Masoud, a Norwegian of Afghan origin in the MOT crew.

We are soon joined by a group of shepherd boys who engage in some banter through our interpreter and Masoud. We share our chocolate and crisps, which they are extremely excited about.

We can hear the rata-tat-tat of a semiautomatic weapon firing down the valley. One of the team says, *"It's just somebody checking their weapon, happens all the time"*.

Almar, the town at the apex of our route, is a complete anti-climax. There is nothing here. It's just a dirt crossroads lined by more single storey mud buildings with a couple of scruffy open fronted shops and a few tattered market stalls. It's a sort of upscaled version of the mud villages we had been through. Made any 'Wild West' town look like a metropolis - not even a tumble weed blowing through the place. It's one of the province's major centres. Makes one wonder what we are doing here – in Afghanistan.

Turbaned men and a very few burqa-clad women drift about. The men gawp at us as though we have landed from outer space. Funnily enough if we acknowledge the men, some respond with a smile or a welcoming gesture. Interacting with females in any way is taboo so we studiously ignore them.

The roads deteriorate on the way back and we bog-in a couple of times.

We are near the Turkmenistan border and happen upon an Afghan Border Police patrol - four men on foot in the middle of nowhere. They have smartish blue uniforms and matching parka type coats and caps but are a bit short on footwear. Two have old army boots, one an old pair of tattered black shoes, and the fourth is seemingly just wearing heavy socks. They say they have not been paid in months.

The PRT guys capture all this and say they will take it up with the local Border Police chief. The PRT are currently facilitating the construction of his headquarters. They are a jolly bunch and three of them pose for photos.

In the end we return safely, having for sure achieved some orientation.

In the evening I am joined in the sick bay by an Icelandic Colonel, who is leading an Icelandic recce party here. Iceland is considering providing a Mobile Observation Team. He describes how they would be especially useful in winter and apologizes in advance for his snoring.

Wednesday

Flight to pick me up is cancelled due to lack of fuel – fuel trucks coming up from Pakistan are stuck in the snow somewhere south of Kabul.

Conduct town patrol around Maimana on foot. Visit new Criminal Investigation Department building, police station and courthouse. These are construction projects delivered by the PRT or with its support. Work goes on in parallel to develop the capabilities these buildings will house. Such as how to investigate a crime, collect evidence, and present evidence at court. It is not just about construction and it is clearly not a five-minute job either. I can't imagine those skills are in abundance here.

Walk round the bazaar. One quickly gets the hang of the greeting *Salaam* or *Salaam Aliykum* (peace be upon you) and the response *Wa-Aliykum Salaam* (peace be upon you too). It is essentially a universal Arabic greeting and can be said with one's right hand placed on one's chest and a big smile or depending on context an air of humility even deference. The Afghans love it – a display of common decency and shared humanity I suppose.

The central bazaar building seems quite old and is one of Maimana's very few two-storey constructions. There are wooden shuttered windows on the first-floor accommodation and storage. On the ground floor, there are open fronted shops with old wooden doors that fold back in sections, sometimes in bare wood and sometimes painted in tired looking blue and green. Awnings on poles provide shade. Smells of fresh bread, spices, raw meat, and meats being barbequed waft in the air. The vendors are universally cheerful and engaging.

Beyond the central bazaar are streets of single storey structures and flimsy market stalls. It seems pretty-endless: with little stalls selling tin pots, cloth, carpets, clothes, spices, teas, fruit, canned tomatoes, cooking oil and, surprisingly, shot guns – lots of them. The shot guns are crude, and one imagines it would be easier to lose an eye than hit a bird in the firing of one.

Afternoon: go with Hanu the Finnish Police Adviser in the PRT to visit the local Chief of Police. He serves us fruit. He tells me how important the PRT is and how grateful the people are for our help. He says, *"all men God puts on earth can leave good or bad memories of themselves, by being here to help us you are already leaving a good memory"*.

With that he presents me with a green and blue striped 'chapan' - the traditional Japanese style of coat worn draped like a cape over one's clothes on special occasions in these parts. The overly long sleeves are mainly for show and are not normally used.

Thursday

Flights cancelled today due to heavy snow in

Kabul. Plan hatched whereby I am to be driven to an RV halfway between Maimana and Sheberghan the capital of neighbouring Jowzan province. A party from Sheberghan would take us from the RV into Sheberghan, where I will then be transferred to a patrol from Mazar-e-Sharif – the main UK location in the North and capital of Balkh province. The UK padre, who is also visiting will accompany me.

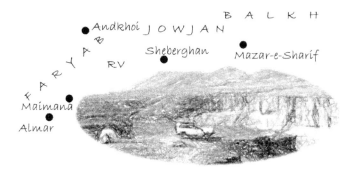

We set off in two Land Cruisers and fuel up some jerry cans at Maimana's only gas station, which consists of a couple of broken pumps and barrels of fuel served from the back of a cart. Weather has changed and it is now very cold with light snow fluttering down.

We leave Maimana on a boggy dirt road travelling east and then to make progress we turn off into a broad rocky riverbed with shallow flowing water. We speed along the riverbed at 40 kph+. Reminds me of 'Wadi bashing' in Oman – scooting along dried riverbeds there.

After about two hours we come out into a village and try to pick up the road again, but we have gone wrong and need to turn around. About a dozen men and some boys quickly appear, look curiously at us, and then direct us back to the road. We pick up the road, but the going is difficult, so we re-join the riverbed when it next adjoins our path.

About a kilometer later, at 1200 hours, the lead vehicle gets bogged-in on the riverbed. The second vehicle gets bogged trying to pull it out. We are well stuck despite much shoveling and winching, both vehicles have winches. The water is icy, and the weather is getting colder. By 1400 hours, no progress has been made so a rescue party of two vehicles is dispatched from Maimana. The Sheberghan party is still five hours away.

Local men appear with long shovels and start

helping. They work furiously hard and jump into the icy water to dig us out. They are as hard as nails. They wear long shirts, some with a blanket thrown across their shoulders, some have wellies or slipper-like shoes, others are bare foot. They all wear assorted headdress, mostly turbans.

It is snowing heavily now, very cold and getting dark. The locals are hugely amused by our predicament. Eventually somebody mentions a '*machine*'. We agree this would be a great idea. Two boys run off to a village two miles distant. Time passes and then a very Uzbek looking character appears on a small motorbike. He haggles over the price of bringing his tractor to the rescue. Fifty USD is agreed, a King's ransom. Time passes slowly and he reappears with a little beaten-up old tractor which we could hear *put-put-putting* towards us in the gathering darkness. He pulls us out, just as the rescue party arrives.

The journey back in the snow and dark is very hazardous with lots of collapsed sections of road and our vehicles sliding everywhere. There are no other souls to be seen, no lights from buildings, total darkness.

The PRT folks are slightly disappointed not to have got rid of their visitors, but hugely welcoming, nonetheless. The Sheberghan party has turned back too and reported in safely.

Friday

We awake in Maimana to bright sunshine and a snow-covered world. There has been a foot of snow in Kabul. No planes today.

We are told there will be a Buzkashi game, so we eagerly set off to see it. But it is cancelled due to snow. We encounter huddles of men around cockfights instead. Normal fayre in these parts after Friday prayers apparently.

Our interpreter and *de facto* guide said they are probably fighting cocks (cockerels) as Andkhoi just north of here is famous for producing them. They could also be fighting Partridges or even Quails. There are several tight knots, each of fifty or more men, packed round the action. Blood sport fancier or not, there was nothing to be gained by trying to join the throng as we would not see anything. Indeed, we are advised that quite such close involvement might not be entirely welcome. Large sums of money are gambled on these fights.

Robert Byron, no relation to the poet, in his 1937 trip report, *The Road to Oxiana,* describes watching partridge matches and wrestling in a field outside Maimana. Maybe this is the same field.

His wrestlers were fully clothed, indeed wore pointy hats, and grapple with their opponent's belt. A form of Central Asian belt wrestling. The Ottoman Turks who originated in Central Asia did this too. It remains popular in the region today, especially in Turkmenistan.

Wrestling is universal. Globally, from the two-hundred-kilogram blubbery Japanese Sumo to muscle packed Senegalese Laamb wrestlers. Timeless too, as Gilgamesh wrestles Enkidu in the five-thousand-year-old Mesopotamian *Epic of Gilgamesh.* Classic Graeco-Roman wrestling has endured, even achieving a famous 1969 'chick-flick' moment in Ken Russell's adaptation of *Women in Love,* when Ollie Reed and Alan Bates wrestle naked.

Camel wrestling, we are told also goes on in this region, especially at Sheberghan. Two of these huge Bactrian things, with humps and midriffs adorned in coloured cloth and bells a-dangling, 'wrestle' until one runs away or is forced to the ground.

The Taliban banned all this along with other traditional pleasures like singing, flying kites, reading books they did not approve of (punishable by death), and generally enjoying life. A short explanation of the Taliban is in the Terrible Recent History 101 at the back.

Killjoy behaviour is typical of fundamentalists everywhere and of all kinds, although they are not all maniacal killers. The Puritans under Cromwell in Seventeenth Century England banned the 'Christmas Festival'. Local councils in Northern Ireland, where I grew up, used to chain-up swings and maypoles in kiddie playparks on Sundays. God obviously didn't want anyone to have that much fun on a Sunday.

We head back to town and have a walkabout in the now muddy snow-melt roads. The town seems much bleaker now in the slush.

We happen upon two Turkic looking men sitting on little stools drinking chai (tea), taking it black with sugar lumps. It is also taken with spices such as cardamon or cinnamon. They break and eat *naan* flat bread that is so fresh I can smell it as we chat. They are a touch reserved but friendly enough given the weirdness of having us foreign troops in their midst awkwardly trying to make conversation.

A gaggle of mischievous boys insist on posing for a photo. In my hometown, Belfast, we would call them *'wee skitters'* (little rascals).

We learn of a dreadful air crash yesterday in the mountains around Kabul (Kam Air flight 904 from Herat, over a hundred on-board).

Another night in Maimana after a long first week. Terrain and weather are shaping events. Home already seems very far away.

Week Two
(Maimana and Kabul)

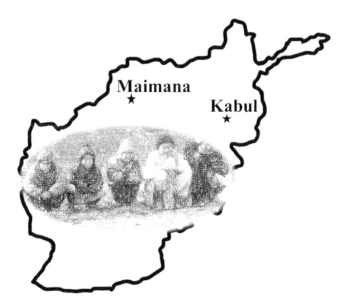

Saturday

A plan is concocted overnight, by which I am to be collected this morning by a UK C130 aircraft and flown to Kabul where I will meet up with my vehicles and Close Protection Team (CPT). The idea is that we all then fly to Konduz with our vehicles and drive off the plane into the town to find the German PRT there. We are then to drive to Pol-e Khumri, the Dutch PRT, and return to Kabul by driving over the Hindu Kush through the Salang Tunnel.

However, we awake to dense fog and news of more snow in Kabul. No flights today. Day spent reading files and papers emailed from Kabul by Robert –

and writing week one diary.

This evening the PRT crew decide I have been here so long that I qualify for a Maimana PRT T-shirt. They duly present me with one over a cold beer. I say a few welcome words of thanks and encouragement.

Sunday

No flights today.

We go shooting. Five Land Cruisers set off in bright sunshine. Roads very slippery due to overnight snow. We bog in a couple of times. The Nordics just shoulder shrug these minor inconveniences and quickly dig out the vehicles each time.

We setup across a valley from a small mud village nestled in the snow. Sound of dogs barking, cocks crowing, children at play, and cackling women is carried to us from the village on the still morning air. We shoot:

MG3 machine gun

MINIMI machine gun

Steyr automatic rifle

SA 80 automatic rifle

G3 automatic rifle

Glock 9mm automatic pistol

Browning 9mm automatic pistol

Children, some of them little more than toddlers, gather to watch proceedings. They are joined by an older boy with a couple of Kuchi dogs. When we finish, they swoop on where we had been firing from and scoop up the empty brass cases. They will apparently sell their winnings for forty cents a kilo.

On the way back we pass men and children working in a field – picking carrots and loading them into huge baskets on either side of a hapless donkey.

Tonight, the padre, also still stranded here, holds a communion service in the briefing room. Packed congregation of Brits, Finns, Icelanders and Norwegians in assorted military and sports gear. I wear combat trousers, timberland deck shoes and a green puffa jacket. The padre leads us with gusto, and we sing heartily:

"Dear Lord and Father of mankind, forgive our foolish ways ...."

I think of St George's Church in Wiltshire where my family worships. Outside our voices carry in the darkness to our Afghan sentries who stand wrapped in coats and blankets, huddled round a few logs burning in the bottom of a zinc bucket. Snow flutters down quietly from the Hindu Kush.

During the night we learn that a group of aid workers have rolled their 4x4 – one killed and three injured. A Blackhawk is to come in and pick-up one of the injured and I am to go out on it. But it doesn't come.

Monday

At last – flying weather – a Portuguese C130 comes into Maimana. I travel upfront with the pilots again. Weather deteriorates further as we fly over the Hindu Kush to Kabul. The pilots can't see through the snowstorm. The tension on the flight deck is palpable as we come in for the landing.

I am met by the Woofer crew who run me up to the headquarters. Turns out ISAF has been assisting the Afghan National Army (ANA) in vain attempts to reach the crashed aircraft. In a break in the weather today a Spanish Cougar helicopter drop a Slovenian mountain rescue team near the crash site. They battle through deep snow to the wreckage and confirm it is highly unlikely anyone survived. The atmosphere in the headquarters is sombre.

Tuesday

Weather severe in Kabul. The Turkish Headquarters, 3rd Turkish Corps, based in Istanbul, which is to take over the operation from Eurocorps, has been unable to fly in as scheduled. They fly from Istanbul and must turn round at Kabul and fly all the way back. This is the second time this has happened.

I begin taking over the job from Nick. A day of office calls and briefings.

Wednesday

Call on UK staff embedded in the US-led 'Coalition' forces. There are currently two foreign force structures in Afghanistan. Combined Force Command Afghanistan (CFC-Alpha) or 'The Coalition' is basically the rebranding of the force that conducted the original post 9/11 invasion. Right now, they are still conducting 'combat operations' in the South and East of the country and run lower-key military operations in the quieter West. They come under US Central Command (CENTCOM) in Tampa Florida.

The plan is for them to be replaced progressively by ISAF which comes under NATO Headquarters in Europe. A NATO command structure 101 is at the back. This was to happen firstly in Kabul, which was done in December 2001, then counterclockwise round Afghanistan. Northern Afghanistan was completed in 2004 under Eurocorps. The Turks will start with Northern Afghanistan and Kabul under their belts (at 1, top left below).

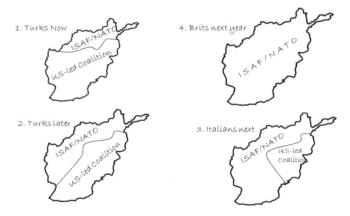

The West would come under ISAF during the Turkish watch (2); then the South during the watch of the Italians (3) who succeed the Turks; then finally the UK hopes the East (4) will be next year under the British-led Allied Rapid Reaction Corps, normally based in Rheindahlen, Germany. It would be the first NATO headquarters to have responsibility for the whole of Afghanistan. The Brits see this as a bit of coup for them.

I call on Major General Peter Gilchrist, the UK Deputy Commander of the Coalition Force. He is one of the UK's more cerebral officers and is a very likeable individual with an easy manner and somewhat professorial air. He tells me he has been standing-in as the Commander for some months while his US boss remains 'Stateside' pending a new appointment. He is very welcoming, and we have a good conversation.

I am still living in the UK logistic base at Camp Souter and commute through the chaos of Kabul daily. Every ethnicity in Afghanistan is present in the city. It is filling with returning people displaced by conflict and by migrants from the countryside looking for work. It also suffers all the overcrowding, congestion, and other stresses typical of cities in developing countries. There are nearly three million people living here. Add to that, it is one of the highest altitude cities of any in the world. No wonder there are air quality issues. If you nick yourself shaving, it can go septic in a heartbeat if you are not careful.

The UK Camp is named after Captain Souter, 44th Foot Regiment, taken prisoner in the 1842 retreat from Kabul in the First Anglo-Afghan War. He survived as he was wrapped in his regimental colours (flag) and thus mistaken for a senior officer worthy of ransom. He had more luck than poor old Lieutenant MacLaine of E Battery Royal Horse Artillery. MacLaine was captured by Afghans in the Second Anglo-Afghan War, after the massacre at Maiwand in 1880. He had his throat cut just before he was liberated.

Thursday

Visit British Embassy. It is in the Wazir Akbar Khan district, named after the Afghan leader who massacred the Brits in their disastrous 1842 retreat. In fiction, it is also the district where Khaled Hosseini's Amir, the protagonist in *The Kite Runner*, grew up. It had clearly been an attractive leafy haven of substantial residential properties, housing diplomats and the Kabul middle class. Sandbag walls, gabion bastions (huge collapsible wire mesh containers with heavy duty fabric liners that are filled with rocks) and checkpoints have moved in, altering the ambience somewhat.

The British Embassy has mediaeval-like gabion ramparts with a formidable double gate arrangement. The contracted guard force are reassuringly efficient Gurkhas. I call on the UK Ambassador, Dr Rosalind

Marsden, for an introductory chat. She is Oxford educated, intelligent, very pleasant and wears a plain loose fitting business suit of grey jacket and trousers. She illuminates some of the broader UK effort here. I also meet some of the other characters in the Embassy.

Afternoon: attend a Counter Narcotics (CN) meeting in the Ministry of Interior chaired by Deputy Minister, General Mohammed Doud Doud. He is a former Afghan 6 Corps (Mujahadeen) Commander who fought the Russians under Ahmad Shah Massoud. He later held out with him against the Taliban in the Northeast. He is 39, energetic and has energized the Counter Narcotics programme.

He opens the meeting by turning the palms of his hands and his eyes heavenward, and with a broad smile amid his thick black tidy beard says, *"In the name of Allah, the Most Merciful, I welcome you all to this meeting".*

We discuss the eradication programme to cut the opium poppy before it is ready for harvest and the disconnect between it and the flagging programme to provide 'Alternative Livelihoods' to the impoverished farmers who grow poppy for their local warlords.

Friday

Nick flies out - I go solo.

The new Turkish-led Command Group arrived tonight. I had met them all previously for a few days in early January during their NATO 'mission readiness training' at the Joint Warfare Centre in Stavanger, Norway.

This is the second time Turkey has led the ISAF headquarters. They previously did so in 2002 when

ISAF was just looking after Kabul.

The Command Group are all experienced men in their late forties to mid-fifties. Smart, clean shaven and in their nation's version of combat dress. Their mood is subdued, matching their Eurocorps counterparts. But they are all glad to be here, finally.

Their command of English is impressive. Most Brit officers have linguistic breadth rather than depth. They can clearly announce in multiple languages, *"Two beers please and my friend will pay"*. I have touristic basics in a few European languages and can *"Kon'nichiwa"* and *"Ni hao"* with the best of them. But have rather lazily not mastered a second language. English, however, has its limitations as the only tool in the box. I always enjoy slightly misquoting Charles V of Spain, Holy Roman Emperor etc on this, *"I speak to my God in Spanish, to my women in Italian, to my soldiers in French, and to my horse in English."*

The Commander of the new regime is Lieutenant General Ethem Erdagi (Er-daa: long a, silent gi), whose daytime job when not in Afghanistan is Commander of 3rd Turkish Corps, based in Istanbul. He attended the Royal College of Defence Studies (RCDS) in London in the 1990s. I had attended it just before my surprise posting here. He is about five foot eight inches tall, of wiry build with greying hair and intelligent eyes that sit behind steel rimmed spectacles. He is good humoured, smiles a lot, and is rather fatherly in his treatment of us all, but steely too. You do not get to be a Three-Star General in the Turkish military by just going around being nice to everybody.

His NATO Deputy Commander is Major General Herman Wachter, German Airforce (Luftwaffe

in German). He attended the RCDS and the RAF Staff
College at Bracknell. He has flat fair hair and small
darting blue eyes. A thoughtful man and something of a
calming influence across the differing national military
cultures in the force. His demeanour is rather serious,
but he has a good sense of humour and is delightful
company, every inch the German gentleman. If we were
in a movie his character would be played by someone
like the late and great James Mason.

The Turkish Deputy Commander for
Operations, Major General Reha Taskesen has spent
much of his career on active duty. He is a tall athletic
type with thick black hair, angular features, and kindly
eyes for such a tough soldier. His English isn't as fluent
as the others, but it is still good and a thousand times
better than my Turkish. He is the strong silent type
anyway, so he doesn't need to say much to have an
impact.

Our 'Air Task Force Commander' is Brigadier
General Danny Van Laethem, Belgian Air Component
(Dutch: Luchtcomponent, French: Composante air),
which since 2002 is the air arm of the Belgian Armed
Forces. Danny sometimes seemed more like a soldier
than an airman in his camouflage gear, but his Aviator
shades are a bit of a giveaway. He looks a bit like Tim
Roth's Mr Orange (the good guy) in *Reservoir Dogs*. He
is full of energy and exudes a 'can do' attitude.

The linchpin is the 3rd Turkish Corps 'Chief of
Staff', Brigadier General Nazim Altintas. Chief of Staff
is broadly equivalent to Chief Operating Officer in a
large corporate. He attended the UK Army Command
and Staff Course in Camberley at the same time as me,
when we were about thirty years old. It would have been

unimaginable back then that we should end up serving together here. Nazim looks young for his years. He is responsible for making everything happen in the headquarters and for managing the interface between it and our NATO chain of command in Europe. In a nutshell his job is to translate the commander's wishes into directives and action. He has a lot on his plate, but you would never guess it from his easy manner. As Chief of Staff of one of Turkey's premiere Corps, his card has been marked for greater things.

In NATO parlance, a UK Brigadier is a 'One-Star' Brigadier General, so I am courteously included as one of the 'General Officers' in this 'Command Group'. A NATO officer ranks 101 is at the back.

We are completed by Suleyman Gokce, the Political Advisor, and at thirty-eight our youngest member. He is an urbane and charming Oxford educated Turkish diplomat. He nearly always wears a dark suit with formal cuff-linked shirt and tie or sometimes a blue blazer with brass buttons. His manners are impeccable, and he has an intuitive awareness of the correct diplomatic protocol in any situation. He is the epitome of the professional international diplomat.

We quickly gelled given the Anglophile outlook imbued by so much higher-level UK education and training and indeed the circumstances – fate has thrown us all together for six months in Afghanistan.

I am pleased to be working with the Turks. I love visiting their country, have some previous military experience with them, and a few polite basics in Turkish.

In Cyprus I commanded a Sector on the UN 'Green Line' dividing the Greeks and Turks. It was not a taxing tour and mostly involved keeping one's own soldiers out of trouble in Aya Napa. I earned a UN medal, a suntan and a Rescue Diver's certificate.

I regularly visited the commander of the Turkish 'Wolf Regiment' in the North of Nicosia. On the stairway of his headquarters was a life-sized mannequin in traditional Turkish military garb. One day as I passed it, I noticed a bead of sweat running down its face. I stared closely – it did not blink or move its eyeballs, but it was alive alright. The rumour was that a Turkish commander could shoot one soldier per year, so I was relieved the mannequin was still there the next time I visited.

Anecdotes aside, anyone who has worked with the Turks in NATO respects them. Turkey is a serious martial nation with a well trained and equipped 800,000 strong army. Their Askari (soldiers) whether from Turkey's crowded cities or the villages of Anatolia stood out for their hardiness and bravery in the harsh Korean War in the 1950s, and not much has changed.

Week Three
(Kabul and Mazar-e-Sharif)

Saturday

I am living in Headquarters ISAF now in my own little 'Corimec' 20-foot container. I have a narrow bed, a miniscule bathroom, a TV, and a phone - paradise. The more junior one is, the more people one shares with. Life for the soldiery can get quite crowded, sometimes even hot bedding with a comrade. I have been there, done that, and lived with other people's smelly socks, snoring, farting, and inability to clean the toilet pan.

Attend Counter Narcotics (CN) meeting in Ministry of Interior co-chaired by Minister General Mohammed Doud Doud and the UK Ambassador, UK is the G8 lead for CN in Afghanistan. The irony of this is not lost on anyone. The Brits went to war with China (1839-42) to force it to continue accepting imports of British opium despite it causing immense social harm. I sit beside the Russian Ambassador and opposite the Iranian Ambassador. We announce a CN Trust Fund and seek donors from all assembled ambassadors. World Bank offers 70 million USD. A good morning's work, but we need billions.

Pop across to the UK Embassy at the invitation of the Ambassador. Some visiting German General is calling on her and she would like me to join the conversation. Turns out it's Gerhard Back, my ISAF boss's boss. He commands NATO's 'Joint Force Command' at Brunssum, Netherlands, under which ISAF's operation in Kabul falls (a NATO command structure 101 is at the back). He seems rather dour and a bit surprised to see me, as indeed I am to see him.

Later, I meet Minister Cetin, former Foreign Minister of Turkey and currently NATO's Special Civilian Representative in Kabul. His office is directly above mine. I am shown in by Lieutenant Colonel Steve Morino his US Military Assistant. The minister gives me green tea and Turkish Delight.

Sunday

Weather is clearing – beautiful sunny day. Views are stunning from every part of the camp.

I attend, as a spectator the 'Change of Command' ceremony between Eurocorps and 3rd Turkish Corps. These ceremonies are a NATO and UN weirdness when command of a force changes from one entity or nation to another. They involve a simple parade with no marching about, apart from a small party carrying the flags of the incoming and outgoing entities. Speeches follow, usually too many. There is normally a reception of some sort for a bit of networking with the key guests, which here includes NATO bigwigs and Afghan ministers.

In his speech, Erdagi mentions Turkey is considering contributing a PRT. This will be great if it happens. Turkey has long had close ties with Afghanistan, including Ottoman era familial links between royal families and periodic military training missions here since the First World War. Being Sunni Moslems too, the Turks would be very simpatico with the Afghans.

I visited the Turkish battalion in Kosovo, in the mountains Southwest of Prizren and Dragash. They were immensely popular with the Moslem Kosovans, especially their circumcision program. The Turkish medical teams did the job in a clinical setting with a dab of local anaesthetic, a scalpel, dissolvable stitches, and cauterization to stop any bleeding, plus an antiseptic takeaway to keep the wound infection free. In many isolated communities around the world, male circumcision is still administered in a more traditional setting, and with a sharp knife.

Monday

Valentine's Day 14th February.

Send email to Dinah. Phones not working – no phone call home. I start getting into the routine of hitting the gym at 0630 in the mornings.

Week is dominated by issues arising from the severe weather generally. Danny Van Laethem urges a maximal ISAF response to help people with what resources we have.

Getting around is impossibly difficult. Our Afghan friends tell us that in these severe winters, the old and vulnerable who die in the high villages are brought out for burial in the Spring.

Ramifications of the Kam Air crash in the mountains round Kabul run in the background. An avalanche closes the Salang Tunnel and results in humanitarian issues. The Dutch PRT at Pol-e Khumri provides some help.

Tuesday

Meet Brigadier Andy Mackay (UK), Commander 52nd Highland Brigade. He is out here on a bit of military tourism to visit some of his soldiers – good for him.

Wednesday

Brief Major General Peter Wall, UK Deputy Chief of Joint Operations who is out on a familiarization visit.

Fracas arises out of a dodgy intelligence report issued widely by a PRT. I pour oil on water and get report withdrawn.

Thursday

Day out in Mazar-e-Sharif with Peter Wall.

At Kabul airport I meet an Icelandic NCO. I know him and his boss from my time in Kosovo as the Icelanders were running Air Traffic Control at Pristina airport there. He tells me his old boss has been out here too doing the same thing in Kabul. Apparently, he had to go home in October 2004, because he and his team went downtown to buy carpets, as many others did, but they were attacked by a suicide bomber. A local and a young US female were killed, and two team members injured.

Incredibly sad news.

We fly to Mazar-e-Sharif in a UK C130. Full flight including UK Customs Officials out working Counter Narcotic issues and a team of US Rangers who are embedded in 209 Corps of the Afghan National Army (ANA). They are what the US call Embedded Training Teams. They live cheek by jowl with the Afghans and both train them and fight along-side them, doing stuff like calling in air strikes if required. When we land, a party of ANA officers greets the Americans like long lost brothers: much genuine joy and camaraderie.

Due to time constraints, briefings in Mazar-e-Sharif are at the UK Forward Support Base (FSB) encampment outside the city, not at the PRT which is in the city. Colonel Russell Beattie, the PRT Commander, comes out to give his pitch.

The FSB comprises the 'Quick Reaction Force' of a UK infantry company (about a hundred strong) with a Swedish Platoon of thirty or so and some logistics. They are the only deployable body of NATO troops north of the Hindu Kush that can help the PRTs, or anyone else, from Badakhshan to Faryab.

The German CH-53G Stallion helicopters covering this vast Northern area are needed to move the QRF about, as planes are so limited in where they can land. The helicopters are based at Termez, a short distance away just over the border in Uzbekistan. They come under German command and apparently need approval from Germany to enter Afghanistan – which of course might not be given in a deteriorating situation. Geographic separation is not in itself a killer issue. But both need a closer working relationship and better command arrangements. Apparently, this has been a running sore for some time now.

The area also has local Afghan Police, Afghan National Police, and Afghan National Army battalions (or Kandaks) with their US Embedded Training Teams. Lots of emphasis placed on relationships with the Afghan security elements.

The flight back is delayed so we seize the chance to drive into Mazar-e-Sharif with Russell. Its population is about 200,000, mostly Tajiks and Pashtuns plus some Uzbeks and smaller minorities of Hazaras and Turkmen.

We travel along a half decent road to the city across a very flat plain that extends northwards to Uzbekistan. Lots of activity. Hundreds of people returning from the Hajj. They bedeck their cars as if for a wedding and drive along pumping their horns and waving wildly out of the open windows. It is a joyous carnival atmosphere.

Much low-level economic activity and enterprise visible along the roadsides as we approach the city. Makeshift stalls of wood poles and scruffy awnings, and rows of twenty-foot containers converted to shops and workshops.

The city centre is attractive with broad streets and paved sidewalks, low-rise concrete buildings of three or four storeys and little shops. Some shops have English descriptors on their name boards.

We stop for a moment at the Blue Mosque, a stunningly impressive mediaeval structure on a more ancient site – it is covered in dazzling blue tiles. General Wall loves it and is having a great time.

Back at Mazar-e-Sharif airport we go into the primitive air control tower there and meet the US Air Force Liaison Officer and some locals. We fly out in a UK C130.

Friday

Snowing again.

PM: brief General Sir Timothy Granville-Chapman, 'Commander in Chief of UK Land Forces', who is out here visiting UK troops. We RV at a 'safe house' somewhere in Kabul and I brief him in the drawing room.

Evening: farewell dinner for Ambassador Angel Lossada, who was the Political Advisor for Eurocorps but stayed on for a bit of continuity.

Week Four
(Mazar-e-Sharif, Faisabad, Konduz and Kabul)

Saturday

Today, as requested by the Commander, I produce an outline plan for training the 'Key Leaders' of the troops who will expand NATO's operations into Western Afghanistan.

We have settled into a 'battle rhythm' around the Commander – as is required in all military headquarters. Friday morning is off-ish, at least there are no morning briefings. Saturday is Monday here, so to start the week the Commander has a big morning update with all the key staff. On all the other mornings there is a quick update for half an hour or so with the Command Group and one or two others. Nazim, as Chief of Staff, leads everyone through all these. The Commander's Brit Military Assistant, Lieutenant Colonel Charles

Comyn, a colourful Queen's Royal Irish Hussar, runs everyone through the Commander's diary and inbound visitors to the headquarters, of which there are too many.

Most importantly, there is an unstated rule that the Command Group (Erdagi, Wachter, Taskesen, Altintas, Laethem, Potts and Gokce) dines together every night whenever possible. This occurs in a small room off the main dining facility with the same food and simple furniture as everyone else, but it is private. After dinner, over coffee, business is talked. Cigars are provided occasionally if there is a celebration, or a lengthy discussion anticipated. Alcohol is generally not taken unless there is a senior visitor present who looks like they need it.

Dinner is where differing views on complex issues can be aired in civilized discourse, or where informal guidance can be sought. They are invariably good conversations and helped forge us as a 'Band of Brothers' who had each other's backs.

Minister Hikmet Cetin, NATO's Ambassador-level Senior Civilian Representative (SCR) joins from time to time. This is always a pleasure as he brings a different perspective to the table.

I also attend a daily morning meeting to discuss any intelligence reports of threats against our troops and installations. It is chaired by Major General Taskesen and run by the ISAF Intelligence Officer, a US Colonel. In the evenings there is a quick operations update on any incidents that have occurred.

Sunday

Frenetic day in the office clearing all the paperwork for the upcoming week as we plan to be away as a Command Group on an 'orientation tour' of the key PRTs in the North.

Monday

We take a Turkish C130 over the Hindu Kush to Mazar-e-Sharif. Clear sky and great views of the vast snow-capped expanse.

The PRT is located in-town in a large scruffy house within a shabby compound – but it has a certain charm. Colonel Russell Beattie gives an eloquent exposition of both the PRT here and at Maimana, which reports through him. He emphasizes Security Sector Reform and mediating local factional disputes. We also hear from the senior civilians there including representatives of the FCO, DfID, US Department of State and a senior Norwegian Police Advisor.

Mazar-e-Sharif PRT

Russell outlines tensions over control of the Hayratan gas station between former warlord General Rashid Dostom and the Provincial Governor, Atta Muhammad Nur. Russell had mediated a tricky situation. Legitimate authority asserted, situation calmed but in Russell's own assessment, not entirely resolved.

Dostom and Atta are old rivals. This prompted a discussion around the complexity of supporting the individual Provincial Governor office holder in the mire of Afghan relationships. Especially as they are appointed by the President rather than elected locally.

We meet local Afghan National Army (ANA) Commanders and some District Governors but not Atta Muhammad who is out of town. We visit a regional police training school and meet the US contractors, all ex-US policemen, doing the training, and a lot of keen, if slightly bewildered, Afghans.

We learn that over 60% of recruits are illiterate so the US has plans to fund a multimillion-dollar literacy programme. The US will have trained and equipped 60,000 police in Afghanistan by October 2005. It also plans to deploy 205 'Mobile Assistance Teams' to mentor and shore up the police. (PRT Police Advisers deal with provincial and district police chiefs enabling equipment and infrastructure projects and advising on operational issues. The MATs would be alongside police patrols on the ground).

We fly to Konduz and get a very formal briefing from the German PRT in a substantial fortress-like location. The military here, led by Colonel (Oberst) Axel Binder, provide physical protection to the camp from which the German aid agencies operate and do not seem involved in reconstruction or security sector reform. They do joint presence patrols with the ANA but do not patrol any great distance from Konduz. There is an impressive small military hospital, which does medical outreach in the local area. We are told the

German helicopters based in Termez helpfully airlifted ballot boxes in the presidential election last year.

The civilian element is not under the command of the military commander except in matters of safety and security. They report to the ministries in Germany that sent them and are here to encourage and support reconstruction based on the objectives in the Afghan government's National Priority Programmes (NPPs). They have spent millions of Euros on roads, wells, food security, emergency relief and schools.

There is no sense conveyed of any integrated military/civilian effort. Each does its own thing reporting back to relevant ministries in Germany – at least that is how it comes across. I suppose inevitably government representatives in a PRT will replicate here the home-country institutional relationships between the ministries that sent them.

We go out to the local hotel for a traditional supper with some sixty local elders and officials. They all look as if they are straight out of Kipling's *The Man Who Would Be King*. An astonishing array of impressive turbans and lived-in faces of every ethnicity. They are all polite and welcoming.

Tuesday

We drive into Konduz. It has a population of about 250,000 and is very multi-ethnic. Surprisingly perhaps, being in the predominantly Tajik Northeast, the largest ethnic group in town are Pashtuns. We walk about in the bazaar. I think this is our Turkish Commander's idea, local German leadership is perhaps understandably not mad keen given there are so many senior officers in the party. I buy a shemagh scarf and

chat with the locals. Met a lad selling warm boiled eggs.
Men carved slices of meat from goat or sheep carcasses
that whiffed somewhat and were hung from hooks in the
dust-laden air.

Our Turkish Commander is brilliant at mingling
and talks easily with everyone he meets, getting down
on his hunkers to talk to anyone seated. They love
having their picture taken and then looking at the image
on the back of the camera. Much hand shaking and a
generally high level of acceptance of our presence.

We then fly to Faisabad. It has a tiny airstrip
closely surrounded by mountains, which make it
exceedingly tricky to get in and out of.

Faisabad is the capital of Badakhshan province
in the far Northeast of Afghanistan. It is nestled between
Tajikistan and Northern Pakistan and its most Eastern
extremity touches China. The Shi'ite Ismaili sect, who
recognize the Agha Khan as their titular head and Imam,
have a large community here. It is a remote region
which grows a lot of poppy and has long been an

established smuggling route between its neighbours.

Osama Bin Laden is rumoured to be hiding somewhere up here on the Pakistan side of the porous border.

We are briefed on arrival by the commander, Oberstleutnant Olef Manhenke. We then meet the Acting Governor, Shamsu Rahman, and local elders who have come into the PRT. They are all astonishing looking gentlemen with fine beards and the grandest turbans.

Tajiks here in the Northeast, and indeed Uzbeks in the North, are not 'tribal'. But there are strong extended patriarchal families and kinship groups dominated by the oldest active male member. The title Khan, which originally meant king and then princeling, was traditionally conferred on some patriarchs of the more prestigious family groups. Family solidarity is everything. Any position achieved, wealth or influence gained, is used to benefit the family. We would call aspects of that nepotism, but here it is just life. Layered over all that is a new caste of 'warlords' who have usurped traditional authority.

We parley with one of these local warlords, reportedly a nasty piece of work, as many of them are. When pressed, he agrees to disarm by the end of April – we will see. Warlords like him nowadays are former mid-ranking Mujahedeen 'Commanders'. Some of them are just gangsters. They have fewer armed followers, and control more limited territories, than the 'First-Tier' Mujahadeen Commanders who ran great swathes of the country in 2001 and are now largely disarmed and absorbed into the government.

We pass a fort built in the days when the Tajik

Mujahedeen under Massoud were holed up here, facing off against the Taliban; see the Terrible Recent History 101 at the back. Massoud was murdered by Al Qaeda two days before the 9/11 attacks. He had the charisma to potentially unite the country, which is likely why he was killed.

Heavy snow is forecast for tonight. We risk being stuck up here for days, so we return to Kabul without continuing to the Dutch PRT in Pol-e Khumri.

Wednesday

Back in Kabul, I attend Afghan Deputy Interior Minister for Counter Narcotics, General Doud Doud's, fortnightly Counter Narcotics meeting. We learn that the UK trained Afghan Special Narcotics Force seized 861 KG of Heroin in the south of the country and 3.5 tonnes of hash. In another operation 560 KG of heroin was seized. The Central Poppy Eradication Force will deploy in a week or so and start cutting the poppies before they are ripe for harvest. It looks like we will have a bumper year for eradication – which is probably fine for the warlords as they have so much stock from last year, they could use a successful eradication season to force prices back up.

Thursday

The Commander's aide, a young Turkish Captain, walks into my office and gives me a goodie bag. It contains a leather wallet, a leather key wallet, a lock knife, a leather note pad holder, a leather-bound pen set, a baseball cap and a cup with a lead attached to heat it from the lighter socket in a car.

I write a Thank You note and give him one of

my books for the Commander '*Command and Combat in the Information Age*', which I had edited and co-authored a couple of years ago.

Attend the PRT Executive Steering Committee in the Ministry of Interior building. Like all government buildings in Kabul, it is extremely crowded. Burqas are banned in the workforce, so ladies are in headscarves. Guards do security checks with one of those airport scanner things that one walks through. If it goes ping the drill is to take out one's pistol and show the guard it is not loaded, one is then nodded through.

The meeting is chaired by Minister of Interior Jalali – urbane, charming, clean-shaven, and fluent in English – he had been a broadcaster for Voice of America. Other Afghan ministers attend together with ambassadors from troop contributing nations, plus UNAMA (United Nations Assistance Mission in Afghanistan), and assorted Coalition, ISAF, and Afghan Generals. The Coalition provide the secretariat function and manage the processes as they provide the great bulk of the PRTs. It is intended that this role passes to ISAF once it owns the majority of the PRTs.

Very high-level conversations in diplomatic tones. Bit of an eagle's eye view. PRTs are clearly just a few tiny bright stars in a vast and complex firmament of other international activities. The Afghans there seem very keen on PRTs and want to see more of them. They stress the acme of their future success will be not being needed. PRTs are to fade away.

Friday

Ambassador Adam Kobieracki, Assistant Secretary General for Operations of the North Atlantic

Council, NATO's governing body, flies in. The Command Group entertain him to dinner. He is a bright and engaging Polish diplomat.

Evening also occupied working our response to a credible bomb threat to the PRTs.

Week Five
(Kabul and Herat)

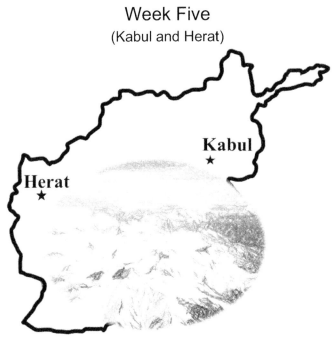

Saturday
Spend most of the day dealing with the suicide bomb
threat to the PRTs in the North, which happily goes
away.
Join in on some of the briefings to Ambassador
Kobieracki.

Sunday
    Accompany the Commander to Herat, sitting
with him up-front in the cockpit of his Turkish C130 for
the 90-minute flight.
    At Herat airport an old man in an overcoat acts
as the marshal and with a few wild gesticulations guides
our C130 onto the pan. There is no safety equipment
whatever at the airport, as far as one can tell, but civilian

flights come and go.

Herat has a population of about 270,000 and is 65% Tajik. It is the most developed and organized place I have seen in Afghanistan thus far. It has tarmac roads, some with a white dashed line down the middle, no potholes and even street lighting that works in places. Modern office buildings with coloured glass fronts and glass fronted shops are dotted amongst more traditional structures. A mix of modern and traditional life fills the streets. It is also warm, like an English summer day. It feels like another country.

There is a lot of Iranian influence, politically and commercially. This is not surprising, given Iran's proximity and that Herat was part of Persia or 'Greater Persia' for much of its history. Indeed, Herat was besieged by Persia in 1838 but was pulled off by the Brits who applied naval pressure in the Persian Gulf. There are a lot of black burqas about as well as the now familiar blue. Added to which the Tajiks speak Dari, a form of Persian.

Almost exactly five hundred years ago, Babur visited Herat as a young man before he founded the Mogul Empire. Writing in his diary, he paints an exquisite picture of Herat as a city with Persian character, great architectural splendour, and tremendous social gaiety. This is in stark contrast to how he frames his then capital of Kabul as functional and multi-ethnic rather than cosmopolitan, albeit in a spectacular mountain ringed setting. The essential differences between these two great cities have changed little over the centuries.

We are briefed by the in-place US forces and then the incoming Italians. We learn, among other things, that USAID and France have funded a burns unit in Herat because so many young girls in the region, over a hundred in the past year, set fire to themselves in protest at forced marriages with older men.

We also meet Consuls from the few countries that have Consulates in Herat and have accepted an invitation to come into the PRT. Rather bizarrely perhaps, this includes the Iranian Consul who is utterly charming. He tells us Iran has plans to extend its rail and fibre optic telephone cable networks into Herat.

He also tells our Italian friends they will be much more welcome than the Americans. He says Herat is quiet from a security perspective. If they have any security concerns, he will use his good offices to help calm the situation. The cynic in me wonders if the Iranians are above creating a situation that might then require the calming intervention of their good offices.

We fly back to Kabul over the now familiar vast expanse of harsh terrain. First, barren rock from horizon to horizon, then nothing but endless jagged peaks covered in snow and ice.

Some of Britain's most maverick characters had walked across the landscape below, either because they were inveterate explorers like Thesiger, or on a madcap adventure like Newby. Insane to think those two accidentally bumped into each other somewhere down there, as if it were Piccadilly Circus rather than an immense forbidding wilderness.

Newby tops-out his 1957 trip report '*A Short Walk in the Hindu Kush*' by reporting that Thesiger, whom he describes as *"a crag of a man"*, called him and his travelling companion Hugh Carless, *"a couple of pansies"* for using airbeds. I wonder what Thesiger would have made of our Corimec cabins.

Much reflection on our trip over dinner.

Monday

Meeting across town with Ambassador Jolanda Brunetti Goetz at the Italian-led and funded Justice Project Office (Italy is the G8 nation leading Justice Reform). I take the ISAF Senior Legal Advisor, Captain Ismail Pamuk, along for the ride.

Their task seems beyond Herculean. They are in the process of helping the Afghans codify applicable national laws from myriad local laws. They must also build courts, prisons, and other edifices of the criminal justice process. On top of that, train four hundred judges, plus prosecutors, court officials, and so forth.

There is also a culture of justice being dispensed by local village shuras (councils) based on traditional and religious codes rather than secular law. The Sharia religious code tends to be punitive – cut off the thief's hand and an 'eye for an eye' – whereas the traditional code tends to be restorative – give back the stolen goods, pay blood money to the family of the killed relative. Both give women a rough ride. An access to justice at district level programme is being launched.

She readily agrees to talk to our Command Group about all this. Justice Reform could turn out to be 'the long pole' in the Security Sector Reform tent. Once the place stops being a war zone, malicious actors need to be arrested by police and prosecuted rather than killed 'in the field' by soldiers.

Meet Richard Hogg of DfID. Chat over coffee in a works canteen of Formica-topped tables and tubular steel school chairs crammed into an ISO container behind the UK Embassy.

Drive across Kabul to the Ministry of Finance to see Ian Holland an embedded UK civil servant helping to get the ministry functioning. Ramshackle building. Chaotic courtyard area of people milling about. He is out. We agree to try again.

Driving around Kabul one notices a lot of men with missing limbs, typically a leg below or above the knee. They have no prosthetics and sometimes hobble on a single crutch. Life here must be unbearably harsh in the best of circumstances without also having to deal with such horrendous injuries. An incredible Italian guy, Alberto Cairo from the Red Cross, has been out here since about 1990 providing prosthetics for these unfortunates. The movie *Kandahar* highlights the Afghan amputee issue with grim black humour.

They are apparently mostly victims of Russian anti-personnel mines. The Russians sowed mines widely and indiscriminately here in unmarked minefields to defend their outposts, or to deny access to ground overlooking bases and supply routes. Some were just shoveled out of helicopters. Cluster bombs also caused unexploded bomblets to be scattered over their targets. All this poses a great residual hazard to the Afghan people. Despite inflicting these horrors, the Russians still lost their Afghan war.

Meetings with Ambassador Kobieracki to discuss Counter Narcotics in a bit of detail. He is intelligent and amusing and a pleasure to deal with.

Tuesday

March already.

Bring in team from Afghan Special Narcotics Force to give Lieutenant General Erdagi a feel for what more ISAF could do to help them behind the scenes.

Recce team of twenty-two staff officers from the UK Permanent Joint Headquarters (PJHQ) in Northwood, London, hit town to plan the move of UK troops into Southern Afghanistan, leaving the North to primarily the Germans, Nordics, and Dutch.

Wednesday

Finally get into the Ministry of Finance – chaotic offices packed with busy people. Meet Ian Holland, Abdul Razique Samadi a Deputy Minister, and several others. Great session. The MoF have a task of mind-boggling scale and complexity. Issues include planning capacity, information coherence, audit functions, and budget cycles.

Pop into Camp Souter to draw from the well of UK information. I enjoy these visits – a bit of British craic and British grub. There is a huge print in the entrance way of Lady Butler's wonderful *'Remnants of an Army'*. It depicts Assistant Surgeon William Brydon arriving alone and forlorn on an exhausted horse at the gates of Jalalabad after the calamitous 1842 retreat from Kabul. When asked *"Where is the army?"*, he famously replied *"I am the army"*.

The retreat was indeed a terrible slaughter, but as we know from Star Wars: *'The Empire Strikes Back'*. The British did, launching a punitive expedition in the summer of 1842. This defeated the Afghans several times, laid waste swathes of their country and destroyed much of Kabul. The Brits then withdrew from Afghanistan. Job done.

The Romans struck back at the Germans in retaliation for the famous 9 CE (Common Era) Teutoburger Wald massacre of three Roman Legions. Their massive punitive expedition killed German people and their livestock on a Biblical scale. They then withdrew from Germany taking with them Thusnelda, wife of Arminius, the German leader. Job done.

Now, here we all are. The American Empire having struck back in retaliation for the 9/11 attacks by Al Qaeda, then holed up in Afghanistan.

Thursday

Frenetic day of office calls. Go to UNAMA to see Ameerah Haq, Deputy Special Representative of the UN. Very simpatico Bangladeshi lady who shines further light on the cat's cradle that is the international effort here.

Join Commander in discussion with a senior Dyncorps contractor who had also attended the Royal College of Defence Studies. We reminisce on RCDS and discuss the Central Poppy Eradication Force which

Dyncorps are contracted by the US to provide.

Friday

One of NATO's military top dogs, the Deputy Supreme Allied Commander Europe (DSACEUR), General Sir John Reith (UK, ex Parachute Regiment) in town. Briefings, dinner, and all that. He is a lively character – good craic and plenty to say for himself.

During dinner, one of the Turkish Generals wisely says, *"In Afghanistan think if we must take the hill now with our own troops, or can we wait and let the Afghans take it with theirs, in five years' time".* Echoes of T. E. Lawrence (Lawrence of Arabia) and the Seven Pillars of Wisdom, *'Do not try to do too much with your own hands. Better the Arabs do it tolerably than you do it perfectly. It is their war, and you are to help them, not win it for them.'* All UK Army officers are supposed to read it, but few do as it is somewhat turgid. The Turkish comment is right on the Afghan money, pointing as it does to the need for strategic patience.

Week Six
(Faisabad and Kabul)

Saturday

Fly up to Faisabad. There is a growing Danish contingent here now and Denmark might take over the PRT in due course. The Danes are keen to patrol further into the province than has been done hitherto. There are also a couple of Croatian Police Advisers adding to the international mix. Major Hamish Bell (UK) is here for a few weeks doing a pilot study on whether and how ISAF can best support Provincial Development Committees, which the Afghans are beginning to set up.

The PRT civilian leadership eloquently describe the gap between Afghan reality and the internationals' aspirations for their country. They point up some of the inherent contradictions in the international approach, not least the paradox in encouraging the Afghans towards a degree of local coordination that does not exist in our own countries. I learn too that the GTZ element (Gesellschaft fur Technische Zusammearbeit, the German equivalent to DfID or USAID) are moving out of the PRT to offices in Faisabad.

I take the opportunity to get a haircut from a local barber who comes into camp and is a dab hand with a cut-throat razor. This is an outdoor activity on a stool with a sheet over my uniform and takes all of five minutes.

We then drive round town for familiarization. It's a provincial capital with a population of about 30,000, mostly domiciled in mudbrick houses. There is a sprinkling of satellite dishes and the odd more modern building.

A little river gushes through it and flows under some plain, but fine old stone bridges. We cross one to the bazaar, which is linear and extremely basic. There is a myriad of little stores and plenty of freshly butchered meat.

In the middle of the town on a prominent riverside spur is the new police headquarters in a rather swanky rotunda-like building. I thought it was a hotel at first, or the den of a Bond villain.

Taking off from Faisabad is always a bit of

'touch and go' as the curtain of mountainous rocks is so close to the end if the runway. We make it out.

Back through the bustle of Kabul in time for dinner with DSACEUR, again.

Sunday

Working breakfast in the British Embassy with Richard Coddrington, Head of the FCO Afghan Section who is out for a visit. I always think a working breakfast is a great way to start a day, mostly because I like breakfast, but it also frees up the rest of the day. Whilst there, I catchup with the Embassy Counter Narcotics Team (a.k.a. the drugs team).

Another dinner with DSACEUR. This time also with a Lieutenant General Martin (Luftwaffe). He has dropped down from NATO's Air Command in Ramstein, Germany, to visit to all the NATO Air Forces' elements here.

Monday

Roundtable at the German Embassy with the Acting Ambassador Dr Rudiger Lotz, a 'panel of specialists' and me. Bit of a grilling really but it went well.

Discovered there, Lieutenant Colonel Gerhard Faustmann, who was described as 'The Military-Political-Adviser' but is the *de facto* German 'Defence Attache' (DA). All embassies have one under normal conditions. It seems a useful idea to have one in Kabul, the Brits don't as yet. DAs usually do two or three-year tours. The right person could learn the lingo, cultivate relationships with senior Afghan military figures and provide a bit of continuity.

Travel across Kabul to see General Sadaad, chief of the Counter Narcotics Police. Traffic is horrific. Once we grind to a crawl my protection team jump out, as is their drill, and take station at roughly each wing mirror. This causes the crowd to spill away from the car slightly and sets up the guys to respond better if they spot a badness about to happen. Safer out than in, I say, so sometimes I get out too.

Back to ISAF after Sadaad, then back across Kabul again to see Brigadier General Patang, the Afghan 'PRT Director General' in the Ministry of Interior. He is a senior police officer. All the Ministry of Interior liaison officers in PRTs are policemen who report to him. I suggest visiting PRTs together.

2230: UK civilian shot and killed in downtown Kabul.

Tuesday
International Women's Day.
Attend celebrations in Kabul Intercontinental Hotel amid huge security effort. Women all look business-like, some are glamorous, some in police and military uniforms. An amazing spectacle given the denial of any public identity conferred on many women by wearing a burqa.

Lots of children there looking great, if slightly lost, in traditional dress.

A banner on the wall reads '*for overall development of the nation, not only men but also women's proactive participation in politics is the way forward*'.

Female literacy in Afghanistan is only 14% - and in many traditional areas attempts to educate girls are resisted, sometimes violently.

Maternal mortality (death resulting from pregnancy or childbirth) is 1,600 per 100,000 live births in Afghanistan, 6,000 in some remote areas. In UK it is about ten.

Over 40% of Afghan women are married off before they are eighteen and a third of those have children before that age. Sometimes girls are given in marriage as settlement of a debt.

An astonishing 90% of women in Afghanistan have no formal identity papers or proof of citizenship.

The Soviets when here pushed female emancipation as integral to Socialism. Georgi Mirsky in *Afghanistan in Our Lives* (1989) says this aroused great antipathy, especially amongst the Pashtun tribes and many other Afghans who '*viewed the liberation of*

women as a violation of the very foundations of life'.
Such deeply ingrained attitudes remain to be overcome
in much of Afghanistan.

So, despite some legislation to protect women
and give them access to opportunities, these brave
women have a fight on their hands.

Drop round to the US Embassy to call on
George White, their PRT Director, who oversees US
Department of State personnel and activities in PRTs.
Their Embassy is a massive fortress guarded by a
battalion of Peruvian contractors and an inner core of
US Marines. Getting into it is quite a feat.

Later George Ferguson calls by my office, Head
Analyst on Afghanistan from the UK Cabinet Office.
Turns out he is Robert's cousin.

Dinner at the residence of the Pakistan
ambassador. A wonderful occasion. I sit between the
Libyan Charge D' Affaires, Mohamed Hassan El-Ayeb,
and the Russian Ambassador, Zamir Kabulov. Former
'Northern Alliance' mujahadeen leaders Ishmail Khan
(now Water and Energy Minister) and Gen Bishmullah
Khan (now Chief of the Afghan National Army) are
among the guests. Food is fantastic local cuisine: spicy
soup and a banquet-like buffet of spicy meats with
naans, water, and soft drinks, followed by green tea.

The Russian Ambassador is great craic, as
Russians often are. I said to him, "*I thought Russia was
chased out of here?*" and he said, "*Oh no, that was not
Russia, that was the Soviet Union*".

As a parting gift, Moslem guests are presented
with beautifully bound copies of the Quran, which goes
down extremely well. A large silver bowl of water and
fresh white hand towels are provided for formal hand

washing.

Wednesday

Counter Narcotics meeting at the Ministry of Interior – we hear that Afghanistan's narcotics industry is estimated to be worth 2.8 Billion USD per annum and constitutes some 60% of the country's GDP.

On return to office, I brief the visiting Norwegian Defence Committee on PRTs. It is a big delegation, so we do this in a meeting room around a long boardroom style table. There is a constant stream of visitors here. I always extemporize without notes and tailor what I have to say to what they need to know and the time available. It usually results in a good conversation.

I sometimes start with 'state building', which is what we have got ourselves into here. It is traditionally a centuries' long, painful, even violent process in which kings, princes, barons, and priests vie for power amongst themselves and with parliaments and people. So inevitably some of the things we seek to help Afghans do here will cause a reaction from threatened vested interests. The societal changes could be immense, so we need to think in generation-long timescales.

Jihadists like the Taliban see modern states as a Western construct with boundaries set by colonialists, and secular rather than religious authority and laws. They especially reject the legitimacy of democracy and ideas of individual freedom and choice. Aid workers doing ostensibly good works can be at serious risk here, especially anyone working to advance women and girls, enabling elections, or generally pedaling democracy.

Democracy is not an easy fit for traditional

societies like Afghanistan anyway. Power has not historically derived from the ballot box. Traditionally, power is taken, held, and exerted through patronage and inducement – distributing 'the spoils' to cement otherwise shifting alliances. In the past, the spoils would have been from raids on neighbours or on passing caravans, or subsidies collected to allow free passage through valleys and mountain passes. But now the spoils are placements, contracts, back handers, a slice of the development action, and increasingly drug money too. How these traditional dynamics meld with democratic political processes and emerging state institutions is very much the tricky journey we are on.

The challenges are immense. But the Taliban failed miserably to deliver even the basic healthcare that the people here clearly crave, and they caused misery and immense hardship. Every well of clean water, functioning medical centre, school, and police post is another nail in the coffin of their prospect of returning. But if they are the nails, the stake through the heart is good governance and a functioning rural economy, both of which pose quite a challenge.

Sometimes all that stuff is the only thing passing visitors want to talk about. I usually major on describing the overall PRT effort in a very general and candid way, telling it how it is, or at least how I see it. If a nation already contributes to PRTs, I always emphasize how important that contribution is and try to bring that to life with specifics that I have seen first-hand. I also encourage them to do more. If not already contributing, I push PRTs as a game they should get into. My overall message is positive and upbeat, while being open about the obvious challenges. The Norwegians of course are massively into PRTs and are major donors to Security Sector Reform and development more broadly, so we have a lot of good practical issues to talk about.

Afternoon: back at the Ministry of Interior for the PRT Working Group (Afghans / Coalition / NATO / UN /various civilian agencies / contributing countries). Afghan led, but Coalition managed, as they do for the PRT Executive Steering Committee.

Total contrast to the prior high-level ESC meeting. Chaotic, even adversarial interface with civilian internationals. Coalition secretariat give a well-intentioned *'this is how it is'* sort of PowerPoint briefing but without any prior consultation. There is a lack of any agreed understanding as to what a PRT is meant to be, comprise, or do; let alone what success might look like. Indeed, there is deep suspicion of PRTs on the part of many civilians in the room.

In fairness to the Coalition, they are still conducting combat operations in the South and East. PRTs there are designed to provide some 'hearts and minds' quick Band Aid projects in support of combat forces, sometimes in the aftermath of action. In the ISAF area combat operations have pretty much ceased. Outside of Kabul, PRTs are the entities through which ISAF conducts its stabilization activities. ISAF's combat forces are its Quick Reaction Forces which exist to support PRTs if they get into difficulties, so it is the other way round from the Coalition area. But there is no common PRT model in ISAF or even a shared understanding of the need for one.

There is an immense amount of work ongoing to deliver Afghan National Priority Programmes and much else under numerous United Nations agencies and bodies funded by the World Bank, Asia Development Fund, donor nations and others. There is a lack of consensus around the table as to how PRTs fit into that, if at all. Charm offensive needed and thinking cap time.

Visit German Police Project Office (Germany is the G8 lead for police reform). They are focused on high level issues such as impartial application of the law, human rights, and leadership training. The US has taken on delivering a large-scale Afghan police force on the ground. The Germans see this as complementary to their activities.

The UNDP (United Nations Development Programme) supported Law and Order Trust Fund for Afghanistan finances police salaries, equipment, and infrastructure. And of course, there are the Police Advisers in many PRTs working with District and Provincial Chiefs of Police. So, lots going on. Policing is the bedrock of effective community security and hence should be integral to any viable ISAF exit strategy.

Out into Kabul again. Pretty much all the guys pulling these heavily laden handcarts are the distinctive Mongolian looking Hazaras. They must be at the bottom of the social heap. When I see them, I think of my dad pushing a handcart around Belfast in the mid-1940s, when he was about thirteen. I don't imagine it was as heavily laden as these things, but it was a handcart, nonetheless. He went on to own a shipping company. I suppose a start like that either grinds you down or makes you a driven man who doesn't take shit from anybody.

Thursday
   Visit Camp Souter and have lunch with Colonel

James Denny, Commander British Forces Afghanistan (a.k.a. COMBRITFOR). British troops in Afghanistan report through him and he provides administrative support to Brits in the ISAF and Coalition headquarters. He is great company, an infantryman to his rock-solid core. He proudly sports a Fusilier's red and white cockade on his regimental beret. Great grub. There is a buffet with everything from cuts of meat, poultry and burgers to spuds done every-which-way. I have Nasi Goreng with lashings of tabasco.

Take a few pics of Kabul including the so called 'Russian Flats' which are what they say they are – flats built by the Russians when they were here. Essentially, a few ghastly ten-storey blocks with washing hanging outside on long lines run out to adjacent trees, now leafless and forlorn.

Back at the headquarters, Colonels Richard Cripwell and David Armitage call by. They are out from the UK Ministry of Defence to see if they can help with 'Information Operations'. That's military speak for 'hearts and minds' campaigns. Colonel Huw Lawford joins the conversation – he looks after these issues in the headquarters. We were in the same regiment and we often natter together. They do stuff like polling to see what the Afghans think of us all. The Brits had polled around Mazar-e-Sharif and found a high level of support for the PRT.

Evening: found the bar at last. Have a glass of wine with Robert and the 'hearts and minds' colonels. The bar has a very woody interior and an outside seating area giving it a weirdly Alpine café feel.

Friday

Salang tunnel still blocked, drive to Pol-e Khumri postponed again.

Office call by a young PhD from Kings College London who is researching Central Asian security and stability issues. She is escorted to the office and arrives carrying a rucksack that looks bigger than she does. Traveling alone, she had flown into Tashkent and travelled by train to Hayratan on the northern Afghan border, where the rail line ends, and then taken a taxi to Mazar-e-Sharif, where she hitched a lift on a UN plane to Kabul, and then took a taxi ride across town to my office. On which basis I assume the security situation is just fine.

Week Seven
(Mazar-e-Sharif, Hayratan, Maimana and Kabul)

Saturday

Office day.

Conceive and get the team working on 'The PRT
Handbook' to compile all the diverse extant direction to
NATO PRTs. With any luck this will help promote a
more common approach.

It is also an initial 'low ball' to get everyone
engaged. We also need more directive instructions to
PRTs and a better handle on what they are doing. Are
they succeeding, who says so, and how is that
measured?

Sunday

Another busy office day.

Monday

Fly to Mazar-e-Sharif with Colonel Pete Curry (US) who works to Nazim and makes day-to-day military operations happen. He's a great guy and I enjoy his company. Spend the day there in briefings with the PRT on upcoming security issues. Session with the NATO 'Lessons Learned' team that has flown in from Lisbon. Stay in gloomy transit accommodation in the PRT compound.

Tuesday

Depart Mazar-e-Sharif at 0700 hours on a German C160, which looks like a small Hercules but with only two engines and a longish tail.

C160

Severe weather precludes it landing at Kabul or at Bagram, the US base near Kabul. It turns around somewhere over the Hindu Kush, brings us back to Mazar-e-Sharif. It then bumbles on to Termez. No flights out until tomorrow we are told.

Have coffee with the Commanding Officer in

the UK Forward Support Base near the airport. We discuss security issues at the Hayratan border crossing. This includes reports of Uzbek border guards being on the Afghan-side of the Amu Darya river (Oxus in Classical times) which forms the border with Uzbekistan. We all decide to go up there and see the situation for ourselves.

The whimsy on which we set off is in stark contrast to Robert Byron's experience recounted in his epic trip report *'The Road to Oxiana'* (1937). There was a Bolshevik force in Termez on the Soviet side of the river then. A few years previously the Bolsheviks had sent an expedition across the river to Balkh to pacify some Turcoman tribesmen. Local officials in Mazar-e-Sharif, and later in Konduz, repeatedly refused Byron permission to go up to the river. Consequently, he left Afghanistan without having set eyes upon the Oxus.

We drive for an hour across flat steppe and then desert dunes. Abandoned Russian (Soviet) tanks and armoured vehicles dot the landscape like dead Daleks. Now quietly rusted into useless hulks, their turrets face southwards. The Soviets committed an Army of over 100,000 troops here. They built hospitals, schools, roads, and airfields to benefit the urban elite and 'proletariat', while at the same time doing what they could to bomb the villages into the Stone Age. They killed well over a million Afghans and made five million more into refugees and displaced persons. They still lost.

It was Gorbachev who pulled out the troops. The logic of that decision is illuminated in the pocket-sized polemic *'Afghanistan in our Lives'*. In the Soviet view, the committal of their troops in 1979 altered the military balance in favour of their client Communist regime in Kabul but tipped the moral and political balance against them. The Soviets found they could not implant 'socialism' in such an intensely Islamic and tribal country. They were bleeding out at officially 15,000 Soviet dead for an intervention that made little sense to their people. Professor Georgi Mirsky wrote *'Well, what were we supposed to do? Send a million Soviet soldiers there? Block the border with Pakistan, which is over a thousand kilometers long? Turn Afghanistan into a barren land?'*

I met an Afghan Army Colonel in 1991, a couple of years after the Soviets pulled out. He said, *"The Soviets should never have gone into Afghanistan. There is nothing there. The place is a graveyard. They ought to have talked to you British first"*.

We stop to buy flatbread (naan) in Hayratan. Our interpreter buys the bread while we in uniform joke with the gathering crowd of locals. We tear and eat the bread – it smells wonderful and is fresh, warm, and salty.

Burqas are noticeable by their absence here. Women wear headscarves. Girls are going to school. Droves of young girls and ladies are in a school uniform of black shalwar-kameez (baggy black trousers tucked at the ankles with a long loose fitting black shirt over) and white headscarf, giving them a slightly nun-like appearance.

The Afghan border post itself was surprisingly well organized. Our unannounced visit causes a bit of a stir. We are shown around cheerfully by the local commander who then walks us up to the bridge. It had been built by the Soviets to supply their troops in Afghanistan. The initial invasion was over pontoon bridges constructed by their military engineers. The Soviets called it 'the Friendship Bridge'. The name has stuck. It is typical of the ironic naming convention of authoritarian regimes that would happily call a euthanasia program 'Sleep Well' or something.

The bridge combined a road with a railway line sunk into it like tramlines. Overhead was a box-girder, Meccano-like support structure running the length of the bridge. On the other side of the river is Termez, where the German helicopters are. So, not far from Mazar-e-Sharif in terms of helicopter flight time.

We talk to the Uzbek guards on the Afghan side of the river. There are only three of them, young conscripts with no Uzbek infrastructure. They point their rifles at us nervously as we approach. But relax as we parley. They have orders to be there and are not for going away or letting us past, nor do they have the means to summon anyone in authority. This was clearly an issue that lent itself to a calm diplomatic solution between Ministries of Foreign Affairs before something goes wrong on the ground. Maybe it is the Uzbek way of telling the Afghans to do more about security on their side of the bridge.

That said, our new best friend, the commander of the Afghan border post did not look like he was about to do anything rash that might disturb his quietude. He invites us to join him for chai. One of his guys draws water from a barrel and heats it with tea leaves in a little pot over a small burner. The commander then pours it into yellow plastic tumblers, stained black inside from many previous chai, and offers us sugar cubes from a little box. We stand drinking it on the bank of the Amu Darya River, the Oxus in the time of Alexander the

Great. We look across it, as he had done over two thousand years ago, into the endless expanse of Transoxiana beyond.

Of course, Alexander was as mad as a box of frogs by then. He crosses the Oxus in pursuit of Bactrian renegades. Defeats everybody. Is lovestruck by the renegade leader's daughter whom he decides to marry. Kills one of his best mates in a drunken brawl at Samarkand. Founds a city, Alexandria Eschate, at the Western end of the Fergana Valley. Then returns over the river to Bactra, near modern Mazar-e-Sharif, to hole-up for the winter.

We return to the UK Forward Support Base near Mazar-e-Sharif airport to stay the night.

Beside it is a somewhat shabby looking Jordanian tented military Field Hospital to which local people come. They are on a strictly humanitarian mission and are not part of ISAF. We drop into it.

The Jordanians report they treat a thousand people a day and that Afghans walk for days carrying their sick children to receive help. We walk around it and watch the Jordanian medics work little miracles. They have a broad range of capabilities from trauma injury through obstetrics to basic immunization. They exude unconditional and limitless humanity. I am reminded very much of the wonderful Moroccan Field Hospital I visited in Mitrovica, Northern Kosovo.

The UK camp is straight out of the Raj – neat rows of pegged tents. Sunset is a special visual treat with the tents silhouetted against the shrinking ochre light in the gathering darkness. A bugle sounds, as it would have done during the time of the Anglo-Afghan Wars, making it all seem totally surreal.

In the evening we sit in the operations room with a can of Fosters Australian lager each. We watch a DVD of '*Gallipoli*' projected onto the briefing screen. It tells of the disastrous British led operation in World War One to land Aussie and Kiwi troops at Gallipoli in Turkey in 1915. Turkey was on Germany's side then.

1915 was the year my paternal grandfather, Samuel, left Canada to fight in World War One with the Canadian Infantry. When on active service, I carry as a totem his tiny New Testament inscribed '*to Samuel, from Mother, 1915*'. My father's elder brother gave it to me. He joined the Merchant Navy when he was fourteen at the outbreak of World War Two and carried it throughout, serving in the North Atlantic Convoys and surviving his ship being torpedoed.

We had been having great craic before the movie started. After its gloomy ending Pete said, "*You Brits sure know how to spoil a party mood*".

Wednesday

Sunrise is a sunset audio-visual redux.

UK C130 arrives. It is to fly to Maimana and then back to Mazar-e-Sharif before then flying to Kabul. Rather than wait for it to return from Maimana, I decide to seize the opportunity to fly there and see the PRT Commander, Stephen Hughes, who I did not get a chance to meet when I was snowed-in there at the beginning of my tour. I travel on the flight deck. As we warm up the radio crackles and the weather reports say Maimana is a *'no go'* due to weather. The crew decide to go anyway. We fly in the small gap between the low cloud base and the rolling hills and hug a valley on the approach into Maimana. We land in a horrific downpour: great pilots.

Hugely useful catch-up with Stephen while all the unloading and loading goes on. Then fly back to Mazar-e-Sharif and on to Kabul.

In the evening we have a dinner in Camp Souter for some visiting Brits - fillet of beef in black pepper sauce and some decent wine – a real tonic.

Thursday

St Patrick's Day today – passes me by. I usually mark it in some way. As a child growing up in Belfast it was a day off school. When I was a Major in my late twenties I commanded 'The Irish Battery' and we always made a big thing of it with a parade and a party. At the RCDS last year, I took the course to the races. In Kosovo, I presented medals to the Irish contingent who'd had Guinness shipped in specially.

Office day catching up, writing visit report. Meeting with Finnish Chief of Defence Staff.

My Icelandic friend whom I knew in Kosovo turns up to run some project at the airport. It was great to catch up with him. We talked about the incident downtown when he was attacked coming out of a carpet shop on Chicken Street. It is carpet-central in Kabul and plenty of internationals went there. Somebody lobbed grenades about the place. Dreadful business. He was understandably terribly shaken by the whole thing. I couldn't help wondering if he kept any carpets.

Friday

In the evening we learn that the flight taking military personnel to Lashkar Gah (in Helmand province) tomorrow is cancelled. I am supposed to be on it.

At dinner, Minister Cetin arrives late and starts to sit at a corner of our longish table. As a courtesy, I insist he takes my seat at the centre of the table. During the meal he mentions he is going to Lashkar Gah tomorrow with the US Ambassador on a US Embassy flight. I mention my frustration at the cancellation of the military flight. He immediately says, "*Take my seat*". An aide is summoned, and arrangements are made for me to travel with the US Ambassador.

Week Eight
(Lashkar Gah, Buzkashi, Bamiyan)

Saturday

Fly to Lashkar Gah in Helmand Province via Kandahar with US Ambassador Zalmay Khalilzad and Minister Cetin, who came along after all. Khalilzad had a close protection platoon of 15 or so ex US services dudes in civilianized military fatigues, baseball caps, radio earpieces, sunglasses, long hair, and beards, and carrying huge black backpacks containing God knows what. They jabbered continuously on their little radios and were clearly ready to over-react to the most minor incident.

Flight to Kandahar takes about an hour twenty. We change in Kandahar from the US C130 aircraft to two US CH47 Chinook helicopters.

CH47s at Kandahar

We then fly West across the desert with an escort of two AH64 Apache helicopter gunships. We fly with the tail gate of the Chinook down and a soldier sitting on it manning a machine gun. Machine guns also poke out of the Chinook's side doors.

About halfway between Kandahar and Lashkar Gah, we fly over Maiwand, where in July 1880, during the Second Anglo-Afghan War, the Afghans massacred a British force.

It was the middle of a bad run for the British. Only eighteen months previously, in January 1879, the Zulus had slaughtered a British force at Isandlwana, depicted in *'Zulu Dawn'*. A few years later, in January 1885, General Gordon died a Victorian hero after the siege and massacre at Khartoum in Sudan by the Mahdi army.

But Empires strike back. The Zulus were defeated at Ulindi, incorporated into the Empire, and their King Cetshwayo brought to England to live in exile. The Mahdi army was destroyed at Omdurman and its leaders imprisoned. The Afghans were defeated at Kandahar, after which Britain took control of Afghanistan's external affairs, making it effectively a Protectorate.

We flew over groups of Kuchi nomads with their tented camps and a few camels. Their way of life is unchanged in millennia and one wonders how they survive in this harsh landscape.

We are flying straight and fast and at about 500 meters. After about forty-five minutes of desert there is a patchwork of green fields and we drop down on Lashkar Gah.

We are there for the PRT opening ceremony. The US has built the PRT at a cost of about 500,000 USD and will occupy it initially for a year or so before handing it off the British who are slated to come in around Spring 2006. There are speeches by the Provincial Governor, by Minister Atmar (Ministry of Rural Reconstruction and Development (MRRD), the Minister of Agriculture, some US military, and finally Ambassador Khalilzad.

Minister Atmar tells everyone he had been phoned the previous evening by the Governor of the neighbouring Uruzgan province who was worried that two hundred families were trapped by flooding and they would perish. Atmar said he immediately phoned Ambassador Khalilzad and within two hours US coalition helicopters were lifting people to safety. He said, "*the people are alive today because God willed it and the coalition is here*".

Children present flowers and sing a song. There are about three hundred Afghans here including twenty to thirty women who wear headscarves. They also carry burqas which they put on as they leave the PRT – back to peeping at the world through the gauze.

I have a good look around the PRT, and a long chat with the command team. They are mostly US Airborne folks, about a hundred or so. Some Special Forces guys are alluded to and are upcountry somewhere. Nothing much seems to be going on in

Helmand, although everybody knows it is quietly growing more opium poppy than anywhere else on the planet.

The commander emphasizes that he has about five million USD per annum at his disposal to spend on quick fix projects to win hearts and minds and keep everyone on-side. USAID would spend even more on larger more enduring projects. He joked that it all went wrong for *"the Brits"*, in the First Anglo-Afghan War of 1842, when they reduced the 'subsidies' they paid to the Ghilzais tribe to keep open the lines of communication they controlled back to Jalalabad.

He had indeed spotted the spark in the tinder box. There was plenty of tinder in it. The Brit's chosen Afghan puppet, Shah Shujah, was despotic and cruel, so they were supporting the unsupportable. The behaviour of many Brits in Kabul was bacchante and debauched. Both officers and soldiers took Afghan women as concubines and induced many into prostitution. This was a source of visceral resentment. Added to which was the vacillating weakness of the Brits' military leadership, which greatly emboldened the Afghans. So, the Brits had it coming to them really.

I sometimes think the 1842 retreat from Kabul is rather over played. It was horrific for those involved. But the deaths of Indian Sepoys in the force would have been inconsequential to the Brits at the time and possibly the loss of British soldiery. The loss of aristocratic officers and diplomats and the suffering of the accompanying British women was more outrageous.

The political fallout was limited and mainly a growing clamour for retribution. The force was primarily the East India Company's, who ran India until

1858. Peel's Tory government was insulated having been elected on domestic issues in 1841, long after the decision to invade, which Peel had described as "folly" when in opposition. In parallel, 'The First Opium War' ran Britain's way from its 1839 outset and ended victoriously in August 1842. Britain took Hong Kong from China, and secured access for its opium and its general trade to the huge Chinese market, which was now forced open.

The Russian threat to India that the Afghan intervention was designed to keep at bay never quite materialized in the way imagined. Perhaps because the Russians knew it would over-reach them, or because despite the debacle and the lack of a permanent garrison in Kabul, Britain retained the influence it needed in Afghanistan and the strategy of making it a buffer state was in fact successful.

Life at home in rapidly industrializing Britain was brutal too. Famously captured by Engels in *'The Conditions of the Working Class in England'* written during his 1842-4 visit to Manchester. There was severe hardship, hunger, and social unrest. Only three percent of adults could vote. The 'Chartist' movement were agitating for universal adult male suffrage, which the government rejected in May 1842 resulting in disorder, strikes and a government crack-down. These disturbances dominated the news in England for the rest of that year. A chink of reform in 1842 saw children under ten banned from working down mines. A few years later (1845-9) the British political elite and Anglo-Irish aristocracy watched a million people starve to death in Ireland, which was then part of the United Kingdom. The Victorians for sure viewed life and the world differently.

Events in Afghanistan were peripheral to the overall course of British history. Blood spilt on its far-off snows and sands did not drain Britain's imperial resolve. It quickly became part of the litany of heroic failures that Britons love to romanticize and retell, without necessarily learning very much from them. Not least about Afghanistan, which we seem condemned to view through the lens of our own colonial experience.

In the middle of this daydream and the PRT tour and chat, a HMMWV (Humvee) light armoured vehicle has an automatic discharge from the machine gun in its little turret. This gives the US Ambassador's close protection platoon its moment of glory.

There is a concrete plinth arrangement against the wall on each side of the compound and a Humvee can drive up onto it to get its gun peeped over the blast wall so that its gunner can act as a lookout. It is in the act of doing this that a Humvee's gun accidentally went pop-pop-pop. Huge but short-lived excitement with lots of security detachment guys running about.

The dust settles and we sit down to an epic lunch at a long table around which we mix with local chiefs. Mountains of Afghan food is piled on it. Men bring fists-full of long sword-like skewers of lamb and dump them in piles on the table. Others appear with heaps of large naan breads carried in double armfuls, pressed against their dust covered bellies. The bread is delivered by simply letting go at the table with a forward jerk of the belly to ensure the avalanche of bread hits the table rather than the floor. Amid all the wonderful traditional food, cans of Pepsi and Root Beer dot the table.

We fly back across the desert, which looks orange in the late afternoon sun.

A great day.

Sunday

A quiet day in the office.

Monday

Today is 21st March – Norwuz – Persian New Year's Day, which is celebrated in Afghanistan.

The Persian year begins with the Spring Equinox and counts forward from there – not in mid-winter as in our Gregorian calendar. The Persian year this year is 1384, as the Persian calendar dates from 622 CE when the Prophet Muhammad and his followers left Mecca for Medina. The 'Arabo-Islamic' calendar does so too, but that is where the similarity ends. The Persian calendar is Solar like ours with 365 and a bit days per year, and the Arab one is Lunar.

Luckily, the Chinese have adopted Common Era and Before Common Era for year counting, or we would be facing chaos. In some calendar systems the world has already ended.

We go to the much-anticipated Buzkashi in the Ghazi stadium, armed with a little pamphlet explaining it all. This is something else the Taliban banned and is now resurging. It is a tough game played on horseback across much of Central Asia.

The 'Buz' is a beheaded goat or calf, slit open and filled with stones. It is to be picked up from within a starting circle and then carried round a flag post placed a few hundred meters away, brought back and dropped in a white scoring circle in the vicinity of the starting circle. Possession of the Buz could pass between teams during that circuit. It need not be carried by the same team or individual, although an individual home run from starting circle to finish circle would cause immense excitement. There seemed to be no other rules.

As in life, victory on any circuit could be snatched from the jaws of defeat, and *vice versa*.

Buzkashi's original 'Tudabarai' form would have ranged across miles of open steppe. There would have been no boundaries and no scoring circles. The Buz would be dropped once free of the swirling mass of horsemen. There were no teams, every man was for himself, anyone could join in, and there was no uniformity of dress.

Buzkashi had now been codified and boxed into a stadium based 'Qarajai' format. There is now a large defined area enclosed by a wall and stadia structures. This codification is rather like the evolution of village football in England into modern soccer. Perhaps even more like the development of the Eighteenth Century Irish 'Steeplechase' into a form of modern horse racing. It was originally a horse race from church steeple to church steeple across the countryside by any rider-chosen route. It is now codified and enclosed on a racetrack with neat fences to jump.

Traditionally, important Khans would have owned strings of horses and would have ridden into Kabul at the head of them with their 'Chapandaz' who would ride the horses in the Buzkashi. It must have been an incredible spectacle.

The Turkish 'Janissary Band' provide the pre-match entertainment. They are brilliant and play a range of traditional percussion and wind instruments. They dress as if they are in the army of some great Sultan setting off to capture Vienna or somewhere.

The teams today are Panjshir who wear red quilted jackets versus Kabul who are in a sort of dark camel colour. Some wear Mongolian looking hats with fur rims and earpieces, others have hats of the type worn by Russian tank crews. Teams line up facing the Buz placed in the white starting circle. I was expecting ponies and small, jockey-like men, but these are big horses and some quite big men. All of them are clearly big hearted and doubtless fantastically able and tough horsemen.

The Buz weighs in at about thirty-five kilograms. To reach down from a horse and pick up such a thing from the ground in an empty field would be a challenge. In Buzkashi you must perform this feat in a mêlée of horses and riders who barge into each other with enormous force.

From time to time a Chapandaz picks up the Buz. He must then ride *'Wild and Free'* around the flag at the far end of the stadium and bring the Buz back, attempting to drop it in the scoring circle.

'Wild and Free'

He does this in the face of massive resistance from the opposing team. They ride alongside and try to wrench the Buz from his grasp. His own team try to crowd the opposition away.

There is no referee riding about blowing a whistle every time foul play is spotted. An official does confirm that the Buz has been dropped fully in the circle. Another chap in a little white Kufi cap and waistcoat walks about in the middle of it all with a pot of white paint redoing the circles.

I have a seat beside the Commander and all the dignitaries, but my view is partially obscured, so at the outset of the game I move forward and join the throng. I sit with my legs dangling over the wall like a local. Every so often the scrum of horses crashes into the spectators, or horses would charge by so close I have to lift my legs out of the way. I have the sense of being at the Circus Maximus in ancient Rome.

Panjshir win – 10 points to 8. Without doubt one of the rawest and toughest games anywhere in the world.

Tuesday

Fly to Bamiyan to visit the Kiwi PRT. Robert comes along, and James Denny joins us for the ride.

In the late 1970s, I backpacked around Europe as everyone did then. I met loads of young folks who said one had to go to Bamiyan because *"the Buddhas are awesome, the hash is amazing, and everyone is so chilled out"*. Now I am going there.

Robert Byron travelled there by lorry in 1937 and describes in *'The Road to Oxiana'* happening upon several caravans of three hundred or more camels in the Bamiyan valley. He was also very disparaging about the Buddhas as lacking *'artistic value'* and being of *'monstrous flaccid bulk'*.

At Kabul airport, we reverse our vehicles into our UK C130 and tie them down securely. Shortly after take-off, we turn into a long, incredible canyon-like valley. It looks like our wing tips are going to clip the sides and it feels that way for a long time. It's like flying down a tight fjord in the *633 Squadron* raid or along some impossible valley in a *Star Wars* movie. We land on a dirt strip and drive our vehicles out of the back of the aircraft to join the Kiwis.

As we enter the camp and dismount, the PRT Commander, Group Captain John Duxford, says to me, "*Just look the warrior in the eyes*". I am then treated to a most amazing Maori war dance and Hakka – as per the All Blacks, except these 20-30 guys are wearing desert combat gear. The 'warrior' out front is bare chested and carries a spear. This is the most incongruous thing.

I am reminded of a similar experience in Kosovo when I was given a bare-chested Hakka by the Fijian police contingent of the UN on their national day. They also gave me a whole adult pig they had roasted in a fire pit. I drove through Pristina with it in the wee hours jammed in the back of a canvas topped short wheel-based Land Rover – its head almost poking out.

This is a Coalition PRT, not ISAF's, and it comes under the Coalition's Regional Command East. A great operations brief emphasizes their low-key presence but early interventions to defuse conflict. Their stated mission is to strengthen security and stability in Bamiyan province to prevent the re-emergence and export of terrorism and enable sustainable self-governance.

They have an integrated military, political and aid effort with representatives from New Zealand AID, US Department of State, USAID, UK's DfID, and the Afghan Ministry of Interior. Each representative leads a line of activity, so for example DfID leads on enabling local Afghan security structures.

All activity is designed to promote a secure climate that creates space for other actors and increasingly puts Afghans to the fore to deliver Afghan solutions to local problems.

There are just over 100 Kiwi military, 10 NZ/US/UK civilians and 40-odd Afghans - mostly guards, interpreters, and cooks. The Kiwis wear floppy hats and conduct routine patrols in pick-ups with machine gun mounts on the back. They cover the more remote areas of the province by establishing temporary forward operating bases with tents and supplies and patrolling from them. They also have a Quick Reaction Force in a couple of Humvees and the communications systems and skill sets to call in an air strike should one be needed. They are impressive.

After a much-needed cup of tea we set off to see the Buddhas, a UNESCO (United Nations Educational Scientific and Cultural Organization) World Heritage Site. Or what is left of them after the Taliban blew them away with tank fire in one of the worst acts of cultural vandalism in human history. Even the Mongols left them standing when they came through here in 1221, although they did kill all the people. Retribution apparently for the slaying by arrow of Genghis Khan's favourite grandson.

As we drive through the teeming little town, we pass a local policeman, "*Good day to you sir*" he says with a Brummy accent. We stop and have a good old chat. He had been living in Birmingham and had returned home here, you couldn't make it up.

There were originally two Buddhas, now they are just huge scars in the rock.

There is a set of steps cut into the rock behind where the Buddha figure had been. We climb the steps. Every step was a different size and shape, which made it impossible to get into a normal going up-steps rhythm. Everybody has their favourite cathedral steps story. This one is mine. I felt as if I had been downhill-ski training by the time I got back down.

We stop at different levels on the way up and

admire the great views of Bamiyan and its little fort. In the town below Bamiyan residents are welcoming their new lady Provincial Governor, Habiba Sarobi - the first in Afghanistan we were told, modernity indeed.

Kids gather to scrounge from us when we come down. One ragged urchin, Fatimid, with lost looking bewitching almond eyes says she is eight years-old and lives in the caves there. The caves had been home to thousands of Buddhist monks before Islamification in the seventh and eighth centuries. Now they are home to Fatimid's people.

We then drive into town. Its population is about 60,000 mostly Hazara. It has broad dirt streets lined by leafless trees, and a mix of single and double story structures mostly of clapboard and timber. Given its touristic past, many of the little shops and restaurants have headboard signage in English and most have glass fronts. It has a certain charm. We stop at a carpet shop and engage in the customary bargaining.

After lunch at the PRT it is time to fly back down that valley again. It is extraordinary flying along it and looking up the sheer mountain sides seemingly at touching distance on either side, all along the valley. Impressive skills from the pilots – C130 'Top Guns'.

In the evening back in Kabul we have a

reception and BBQ in the headquarters garden for the Supreme Allied Commander Europe (SACEUR), General James L Jones US Marine Corps. He is responsible for the oversight of all NATO military operations.

Wednesday

A busy day in the office getting ready for my ISAF PRT conference tomorrow. Many of the delegates arrived today and so time is spent socializing with them.

Learn today that I passed my Kings College London Master's degree with Distinction.

Great chat with Dinah.

After dinner with the PRT crew I drop in on the Commander and other Generals in the VIP dining room. They are having a glass of wine – it's Herman Wachter's birthday. I add my good news.

Thursday

ISAF PRT Conference all day – phenomenally successful. Much mutual understanding even a degree of camaraderie generated, and some useful basics agreed upon. Draft PRT Handbook well received.

Take them all out to dinner in a restaurant, which is a novelty for us all. It is in a compound with armed guards and the trip is planned like a military operation. We wear uniform. The restaurant has solid wood tables, proper dining chairs, and a menu in English. They cater for the diplomatic and press corps and no doubt Kabul's middle class.

Four US soldiers killed by a landmine in the South of the country today.

Friday

Busy office day. Lots of Counter Narcotics activity going on.

A fatwa has been issued against growing poppy and a five-year Afghan strategy developed. Provincial Governors lead local poppy eradication efforts. Verification teams confirm their eradication. The Central Poppy Eradication Force is cutting poppy too. Aerial surveillance and commercial satellite imagery help identify poppy fields and support verification.

The Afghans have an Afghan Special Narcotics Force, a Counter Narcotics Police Force of Afghanistan, a National Interdiction Unit, and Mobile Detection Teams. A special court and prison for narcotics cases is nearing completion in Kabul.

A Counter Narcotics Trust Fund has been established. International donors can choose to contribute to either Enforcement or Alternative Livelihoods or both.

A lot of funding has been provided to Alternative Livelihoods, but delivery is not keeping up. This is becoming the killer issue for CN.

ISAF is shifting its perspective from looking at NATO guidance and stressing what it *cannot do*, to stressing instead what it *can do* within the guidance. Consequently, behind the scenes support activities are increasing.

NATO and other countries could still do more to assist through donor funding routes or help in kind to develop specialist Afghan police capabilities.

At home, they could aggressively address heroin demand reduction and see such efforts more in the context of stabilizing Afghanistan, which is just the supply end of the problem. They could also perhaps open their markets to Afghan agricultural produce and subsidize a get to market strategy.

Going after warlord money, if it is in a banking system somewhere, is all part of it too. Maybe we need to help these guys get their money out of drugs and into hotels and casinos.

Week Nine
(Kabul and Herat)

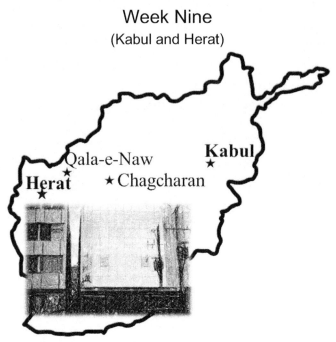

Saturday

Day of briefings and meetings with the Lithuanian Recce Team. They are putting a PRT into Chagcharan, which is one of the most isolated places on earth. It is in broadly the same parish as the Minaret of Jam, which is Afghanistan's second World Heritage site and rarely seen by outsiders. Rory Stewart describes it in *'The Places in Between'*, his trip report of his 2001 solo walk across Afghanistan, *'It rose two hundred feet, sixty-one meters, in a slim column of terracotta set with a line of turquoise tiles. There was nothing else'*.

He also reported locals were pillaging artifacts and materials from the site. He came down firmly on the side of archeological debate that posits the site as the lost mediaeval capital of the Ghorid Empire, sacked by

Genghis Khan, and reduced to sands blown away in the wind. I doubt I will get to see the Minaret as a collateral benefit of this enterprise, as I will be long gone when they inflow. Perhaps the Chagcharan PRT should be the first one to have an archaeologist in the crew.

The Lithuanians were meant to go to Qala-e-Naw, which is only a three-hour drive from Herat, but they got bumped out by the Spaniards who leveraged their promise of helicopters and other assets for the Forward Support Base in Herat to get Qala-e-Naw rather than Chagcharan. They then met their Forward Support Base commitment in Herat by moving their helicopters and other support assets from Kabul, leaving fewer resources available for ISAF centrally.

Sunday

Easter Sunday.

Wonderful sunny day for our trip to Maimana with the Commander. I phone the PRT. They tell me it snowed overnight but the runway is clear. We go to the airport in convoy to find Portuguese pilots refusing to fly. Their meteorological report says it's minus 6 Celsius in Maimana and they cannot land. I phone the PRT again. They confirm they are standing on the airfield and it is serviceable. Pilots cannot be moved.

We return to camp and sit in the Easter sun drinking coffee before scuttling into our offices for a day of word processing and phone calls.

Monday

Small explosive device goes off today and hits a Canadian Land Cruiser. Judging by the photos the occupants were lucky it was armoured. Coincidentally, my armoured Land Cruiser arrives later in the week, thanks to Peter Gilchrist who said I should have one as I beetle around Kabul so much.

I cross town for a meeting in the Afghan Ministry of Interior. I am driven by my new Gurkha crew who have been allocated to me from the battalion that is just rotating into Camp Souter. They find it – no worries. I need the crew to do that as I spend so much time texting and jabbering.

I am there to see the leadership of the Border Police, which is part of the Afghan National Police. They describe the immense scale of the border policing task. Geography: 5,500 kilometers of porous borders in harsh terrain. Tribes: whose traditional lands straddle a border they do not recognize, especially the British imposed 'Durrand Line', which forms the border with Pakistan. Nomads: that roam back and forth with the seasons. Other entry points: like airports, and issues around infrastructure, leadership, and training.

I mention the little patrol I met in Faryab. There is concern but no surprise. Getting pay to individuals is extraordinarily difficult in a country without a functioning banking system or individual bank accounts. I tell how in Nepal the UK sends out a Paymaster every summer to trek round the villages paying out Gurkha pensions. Even as I spoke, I realized that in this country an outsized armed escort would be required.

As a Subaltern, when British soldiers were still cash paid, there were 'Pay Parades' on Thursdays to hand over the carefully counted out and registered cash. One felt like a Centurion handing out salt. Here, one wonders how to confirm with any confidence who got what cash, if any, and when. So many cannot sign their own name and just make a mark. They would need to be taught to write or have their fingerprints taken – neither would be a five-minute job. The American literacy programme for the ANP will no doubt help with this.

Tuesday

Office based day today. I have meetings with various staff members who are doing projects on my behalf.

Lunch with Minister Qaderi – the Minister for Counter Narcotics (General Doud's boss).

In the evening I brief a team of US civilian and military folks from the Pentagon. They are extremely interested – looks like PRTs in some form might be introduced in Iraq.

Wednesday

Emails from home tell me my family is having a tough time – Easter and no daddy.

Presentation this morning on the four Dutch F-16 jet fighters that have arrived to replace the Dutch Apache helicopter gunships that will return to the Netherlands on 1st April.

The Dutch Apache force is overstretched due to its commitment in Iraq. Every nation here that has troops in Iraq has become focused on that as a military priority.

The Netherlands has sent out a Brigadier General to be the National Contingent Commander as they now have: a PRT in the North at Pol-e Khumri; Special Forces in the South; F-16s in Kabul; and plans for a reinforcement battlegroup to come in for the election period; and possibly a second PRT in the South. That's a lot for them, or indeed anybody really.

Attend PRT Working Group. It agrees to develop a standing Afghan-led inter-agency PRT Office to support policy level issues like whether PRTs should be doing more or doing less.

Surprise visit to Kabul by 'First Lady' Laura Bush. She meets Afghan women and urges support for women's rights. Huge stir. She brings Margaret Spelling, the US Education Secretary, in her wake and a seventeen million USD commitment to build an American University in Kabul. Must have been a massive headache for the Security Service guys. Well done her.

Reports of two rockets fired at Herat airport.

Thursday

The entire Command Group and substantial entourage of key staff officers and aides escape to Herat for the PRT Change of Command Ceremony from the US to Italy.

A beautiful sunny day. Herat has a decent runway, so we use the Commander's Turkish C130. We fly for one and a half hours over the Central Highlands and then drop down into Herat.

We are escorted from the airport by four US Humvees. There are so many of us we travel in a large single deck bus akin to what in the UK military we call a 39-seater. We pass the odd smart hotel and modern houses dotted amongst the more traditional buildings. Three-bedroomed apartments in one condo are reportedly being sold for 30,000 USD each.

Our bus breaks down just short of the PRT and we walk the last couple of hundred meters.

The Italians inherited a great PRT from the US and invested in it to make it very impressive. They have polished wood furniture and chandelier lighting to die for - a bit of Italian style in Afghanistan. Perhaps more like a consulate that a military outpost.

We meet the ebullient Brigadier General Giuseppe Santangelo, who is ultimately to become Regional Area Coordinator West. NATO realizes it needs a small headquarters to run military activity in each of its vast regions, but the nations contributing troops and assets could not agree to them being put under a regional 'commander' who has the authority to direct. They could only agree to a 'coordinator' who has the authority to say, *"please could you"*. Giuseppe finds this a frustration, which I share entirely.

He and I get on well. He says I must come to Herat for a longer visit and be shown around. Sounds great. He introduces the very jolly Colonel Aldo Guaccio, the incoming Italian Herat PRT Commander.

The parade starts late because the US Ambassador has not shown up. My Commander makes noises about getting on with it. He says he must go at 1400 hours. The Italians have sent over their Chief of

Defence, who is a Four-Star Admiral, and two Three-Star Generals. They and their aides all wear new Armani styled desert gear that has never been worn before, Ray-Bans, and Toni and Guy hairdos. They insist on waiting for US Ambassador, Khalilzad, who eventually shows up. The parade starts late and lasts too long – too many speeches, especially with translation. The heat is insufferable and we all drip sweat that falls onto the ground in great droplets. One Italian on parade faints.

At 1400 hours my Commander gets up and leaves. Everybody who needs a lift to Kabul in his plane, including the Italian Ambassador, has no choice but to leave too. We all depart.

Friday

April Fools' Day. My favourite was Belize, November 1985. We were helicoptered deep into the craggy jungle at Little Quartz Ridge in the far South and were to be lifted out again, but the helicopters didn't come. We were told they had gone to Columbia on disaster relief. It felt like an April Fools' joke. It then took one and a half days to walk out, cutting our way through the thick jungle. Great craic.

Anyway, back in Kabul I am having a chilled-out day: gym, office, meeting with a Finn.

Early evening: a beer to say farewell to my Woofer (Wooster and Sherwood Forester) drivers and protection team.

Later: a BBQ in the ISAF garden laid on by the Political Advisor, Suleyman Gokce.

Week Ten
(Salang Tunnel, Pol-e Khumri, Dahani-i-Ghori)

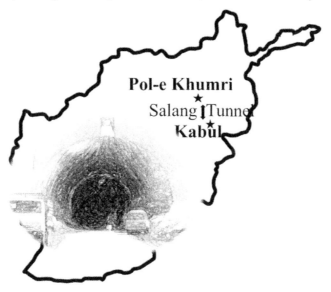

Pol-e Khumri
Salang ↕Tunnel
Kabul

Saturday

Two rockets fired over the German PRT at Faisabad –
nobody hurt.

Orders and briefings for our journey tomorrow
over the Hindu Kush and through the Salang Tunnel to
Pol-e Khumri.

We are told the drive will take 6 to 12 hours
depending on conditions. The tunnel's altitude is over
11,000 feet (about 3,400 meters), which is high enough
to get sick at. Luckily, we are already acclimatized to
5,900 feet (about 1800 meters) in Kabul.

Dreary briefing from the intelligence staff
makes the whole thing seem ill-conceived. They
cheerfully remind us of the Soviet mishap there in

November 1982 when, following an accident and fire, they lost 200 troops mostly to suffocation in the unventilated tunnel. Western media reported 2-3,000 dead which seems improbable. It has been closed due to damage and disrepair and was just reopened in 2002.

There is some concern that I as a General Officer am doing this. In truth, I have become infected with Robert's ambition to go through the Salang Tunnel.

A compromise plan is agreed, whereby I drive up but fly back on Tuesday with our Commander who is to visit Pol-e Khumri that day; leaving the rest of the party to drive back per Plan A.

Sunday

We (that is myself, Robert, some key staff officers who have been working PRT issues, drivers, and my Gurkha team) set off in glorious sunshine. The Gurkhas look very business-like and draw a lot of praise from the international staff officers who find their presence reassuring.

We drive north across the arid Kabul plain passing miles of de-mining activity along the roadside by the HALO Trust (Hazardous Area Life-support Organization). Men prod the dirt with sticks in a technique I am told is no longer used elsewhere.

We stop for a quick break by a walled farmstead that looks like a little fortress. Outside it there is an abandoned and wheelless hulk of a Soviet armoured reconnaissance vehicle and a little red tractor.

We then head up into the rocky hills. We cross
small bridges of the type put down by military
engineers. We soon get above the snowline.

Suddenly, we can see the scar of the Salang
Tunnel approach road running along the mountainside. It
is a long concrete shelter-like structure with an open
side. We turn into the approach – it is full of rutted ice.

We squeeze into the tunnel itself. It is three
Kilometers long, totally unlit, pitch dark and with
insanely deep ruts of hard ice. Our headlights beam like
torches, but we move crabwise in the ice, so they are
often pointing sideways. There is a procession of
oncoming sliding lorries often with no headlights. Horns
blare in a continuous din. The deep ruts almost throw us
onto our sides. Everyone in the tunnel seems out of
control. It feels like a long time driving through.

Finally, we emerge directly into bright sunshine
on the north-side which has no covered approach, so the
sunburst is immediate and a great relief. Lorries are
dotted about waiting to enter the tunnel and it all feels
rather normal.

I am pleased with my new Gurkha team
especially Corporal Sudendra the team leader and
Private Durgahang my driver. We stop and Klaus, a
German staff officer in the 'Planning' section, radios the
base in Kabul on our satellite link to say we are through.

On the northern side, once down below the
snowline, the valley was noticeably lush with

functioning irrigation, healthy looking livestock, green fields, fruit trees, tidy farms, and satellite dishes. It feels like a different country.

We arrive safely at the PRT after an eight-hour drive from Kabul. We are welcomed by the energetic and focused Colonel Theo Rikken and the engaging Dutch Foreign Affairs representative.

We go straight into a series of briefings on the PRT. We break to be treated to an amazing mixed grill of spareribs, steak, and all the trimmings. I then have a mission briefing for tomorrow's patrol. The idea is to visit a village hit recently by a flash flood and to call on the District Chief of Police.

Sleep like a log.

Monday

Drive to Dahani-i-Ghori, park on the edge of the village and walk in. We are shown about by village elders who have the history of the world etched in their faces. A gang of kids swarm around us. An old man is running a little shop by the village spring. He has the grandest white beard and an impressive tidy turban.

He was great. He said, *"Have you come to help or just to look?"* which put all of us on the spot. The PRT initiated a plan to provide Swiss style flood defences that would help prevent reoccurrence.

Women and boys come to take water from the spring which is full of fish. The women wear headscarves wrapped across their faces and groups of them peep out from compound doorways. They peer curiously at the female NCO in our patrol – she is in uniform, has uncovered blonde hair, and is giving instructions to the male members of her team.

There is a half-buried Russian tank in the middle of the village. A crowd of girls appear on their way home from school. There are so many children and so few schools and teachers in Afghanistan, that children go to school in shifts. We give one little boy, Lal Mohammed, a piece paper and he makes the most fantastic airplane dart. It flew beautifully. My young sons would have loved it. He said he was going to be an engineer.

We arrive at the police station - a single story, mudbrick building with a flat roof on which tall weeds grow.

A small central doorway has a window either side and school chairs propped against the wall. We enter and find the Chief of Police at his desk having lunch in his civilian clothes of a shalwar kameez (baggy trousers and a loose-fitting long shirt), open waist coat and Pakol hat. His office is clean and tidy and in front of his desk is a long low table and simple chairs. We are invited to sit and drink the customary chai. He joins us.

He says he has only one vehicle for himself and his 60 men in the vast district he is responsible for. It is parked outside and looks as though it might not start. He also says his main policing challenge is the kidnapping and abuse of young men and boys, often by mullahs.

He then puts on his best uniform and we all pose for photos outside, after which he returns to his office.

We walk about in the local bazaar. It is stinking hot and terribly busy. I am completely thronged by people crowding in on me. They complain about Central and Provincial government and petty corruption impacting their daily lives. I communicate through my Gurkhas. Thanks to Bollywood they and many folks in Afghanistan have a smattering of Hindi.

I am shown a prize fighting partridge in a little wicker cage and made to understand what an enormous privilege it is to see such a thing. I beam genuine enthusiasm. I wonder who has the better deal – this little fellow or its UK cousins living in the wild before somebody has a go at shooting them? I decide this random thought is best left unsaid on my side of the Hindi bridge.

I am offered and accept skewers of meat from one vendor and bread from another – they smell wonderful and taste delicious. They refuse payment. The little crowd closes in quite tightly now. I can smell their sweat and clothes. The Gurkhas are a touch anxious.

A chap emerges as a spokesman amongst them. He is wearing a suit jacket and a little Karakul sheepskin hat of the sort that President Karzai is often seen in. These are expensive and obviously a symbol of authority in these parts. I feel somewhat underdressed in the floppy desert hat we wear up-country. His presence causes us to be given more space. He reiterates the message on corruption which he asks me to convey to Kabul. I say I will, and everyone seems extremely pleased. Smiles all around.

Next, the girls' school which has lost its compound wall all along one side where the torrent swept away the foundations.

The roof of the rather bleak looking boys' school next door had been made unsafe by the rain and flooding. They are now using tents provided by the United Nations High Commissioner for Refugees (UNHCR). Tents will only do for the summer. A makeshift school "bell" hangs ready to ring out and send children scurrying for their seats.

We are also shown a new clinic. The little building looked amazing relative to everything else. We are told it will soon be a going concern. It is the pride of the community and a beacon of hope.

Tuesday

Surprise, surprise – no helicopters. The weather has closed in. I set off on the return road journey with the team in blindingly heavy rain. We drive up into the mountains. Huge trucks lumber up the road with boys hanging on the side of their cabins, feet perched on the running boards or steps, watching for the drivers whom they direct through an open window.

At last, we drive out of the weather, up above the clouds, and into sunshine. Then into the dark Salang Tunnel and the rutted ice in which we are now more confident. The return journey was a breeze after the tunnel. It took just over 6 hours overall from the PRT.

Wednesday

Office day.

Meeting with some Brigadier-Generals from NATO Headquarters in Mons and Brunssum. We discuss intelligence matters.

Later, meet with the British Embassy 'Drugs Team' who run the UK input to the Counter Narcotics effort.

Thursday

Plans to visit Mazar-e-Sharif to see Governor

Atta Muhammad are cancelled due to a sandstorm.

In the evening I retire early and start throwing up. Probably a reaction to the malaria pills for the Pol-e Khumri trip that I am still taking for the requisite days afterwards. I've had a bad reaction before, so won't be taking them again. Trouble is, if you rely on mosquito nets, I always think it's like the Sigourney Weaver character, Ripley, in *Alien* thinking she was safe once inside the escape pod, but the creature is already in there with her.

US CH47 Chinook helicopter crashes in a sandstorm near Ghazni, Southwest of Kabul, killing all 18 on board.

Friday

Feel sick as a dog all day long. Meet some folks from the Canadian Embassy.

Week Eleven
(Kabul, Konduz, Pol-e Khumri)

Saturday

Peter Gilchrist invites me over to the US-led Coalition headquarters. I join discussions with him and his US team on PRT aspects of US exit strategy. They are briefing Washington later in the week.

The Italian headquarters that are slated to take over ISAF in August are in town. Lots of time devoted to briefing them and showing them around.

Sunday

Quiet day.

Morning: brief the Italians on PRTs. Goes down extremely well. I share Afghanistan's traditional 'Three

Phase' wars, which doesn't freak them out too much.
Also explain the PRT paradox that the light touch looks
vulnerable but might not provoke the reaction that a
more robust military presence would.

Afternoon: brief the Commander on my
thoughts for more directive instructions to PRTs and an
ISAF PRT Office with a strong civil component. He is
supportive but is concerned too that PRTs are not robust
enough to manage a deteriorating security situation.

Monday

Office day.

George White from the US Embassy calls by.
He covers US Department of State PRT activities. He is
with Mike Metrinko who is a total legend in US Foreign
Service circles. Mike speaks Farsi and Dari and has had
recent postings in Kabul, and Herat. He was in Tehran
when the Iranians seized the US Embassy there in 1979
and was one of the hostages taken captive for fourteen
months. An amazing individual. He is one of the very
few people who has any real idea as to what is going on
here.

For my part, the more I find out, the less I know.
I feel like Socrates who reportedly said, *"All I know is
that I know nothing"*; especially after talking to
somebody like Mike.

Evening: working BBQ with the Italians.

Tuesday

Absent a taxi service, we in the Command
Group run our Italian counterparts about. Their Deputy
Commander is a Brit and I get to run him across to the
UK Embassy to meet the Drugs Team.

Wednesday

Fierce rain. Lieutenant General David Judd, from our superior headquarters in Brunssum, is meant to be visiting today. He was transiting through Termez and is stranded there by the foul weather.

Prospects for people in the hills and on the floodplains do not look good – much contingency planning.

Thursday

We awake to sunshine. Plan is to fly to Konduz to meet David Judd and join him for his trip to the Dutch PRT at Pol-e Khumri. Nazim comes along too. Our plane is late taking off. We arrive in Konduz airport too late to join him for the Konduz leg of the visit, so we wait at the airport to join the Pol-e Khumri leg.

We take the opportunity to visit the new fort the Germans are building by the airport - we are told it is for their PRT and logistics at a cost of 30 million Euros. It is enormous. This must surely distance the PRT from the people, who live in Konduz, not at the airport. Conversely, if the security situation is so serious that we need a fort like this, does a PRT make sense?

The fort overshadows the adjacent and pitiful Afghan National Army compound of tattered tents with a barbed wire perimeter. A miniscule investment could transform it, greatly enhancing ANA capabilities and no doubt increasing their disposition to protect the PRT.

David Judd arrives. I worked with him when he was a Brigadier and I a Lieutenant Colonel. He is as personable as ever and takes a great interest in everything. He brings with him his Political Advisor,

Maarten de Sutter, who I knew in Kosovo. Maarten has a shock of white hair and is always good craic.

We fly to Pol-e Khumri in two German CH-53G helicopters.

CH-53G at Konduz

They fly at 5 to 15 meters altitude and speeds of 110-140 knots (over 200 kph). It is a great ride, but they scare and scatter livestock. It is only a matter of time until an angry farmer has a pop at one - they all have weapons or easy access to them.

We land beside the PRT and go inside for the usual briefings – which Theo Rikken does brilliantly.

We drive around Pol-e Khrumri and walk through the bazaar. A very jolly tailor with several little 'Singer' sewing machines makes waistcoats for 200 Afghanis *"For you sir"*, he said, *"50 Afghanis"* – about a dollar.

Another wanted to sell me a burqa. Some had magnificent trays laden with displays of brightly coloured spices or fresh fruit and vegetables. Nazim has a great time and tries on some local Pakol hats.

We fly back to Konduz over green fields and woodlands and catch a C130 to Kabul.

Evening: special Command Group dinner for David Judd – good craic and a couple of glasses of wine.

Friday

Office day: briefing David Judd on PRT matters and discussing life in general. Receive office call from some bonny folks in the UK intelligence community.

Week Twelve
(Kabul and Bagram)

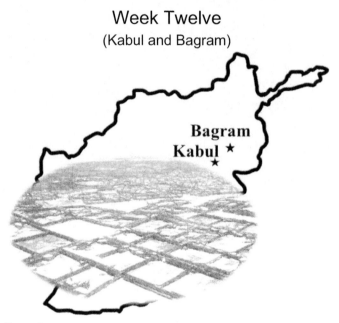

Saturday

Meeting with the Slovenian Minister of Defence, who was escorted by my Slovenian Royal College of Defence Studies colleague, Renato Pietric. Office call by Consul Yuichi Inouye of the Japanese Embassy who explains that Japan is thinking of contributing to the civilian component of a PRT.

Visit Camp Souter. Always a good stop for a decent mug of coffee. The Camp is a weirdly British island. Some folks post supposed Afghan proverbs above their desk spaces:

'The First Englishman comes to look; the second Englishman makes a map; the third Englishman brings an army – so it is best to kill the first Englishman'. Good advice to indigenous people experiencing first contact, even if it is apocryphal.

'Never undo a knot with your teeth if you can undo it with your fingers'. Which is great advice for anyone thinking of military interventions anywhere.

'There is a boy across the river with a bottom like a peach, but alas I cannot swim'. Which I take to mean it is too late to prepare for an opportunity after it has arisen. Dodgy provenance though. John Masters says it is the opening lines of a famous Pathan song *Zakhmi Dil*, or *Wounded Heart*. He mulls over it in *'Bugles and a Tiger'* which recounts his experiences fighting Pathans in the Northwest Frontier in the 1930s. Many Pashtu poems and songs were adapted as marching songs in the Raj and so the original Pashtu version might have been about a girl. *Flashman,* George McDonald Fraser's racist and cowardly anti-hero, sings it in Pashtu about a girl in the eponymous novel. He does so at night to hoodwink a Pathan patrol into letting him pass. So, if the original had been about a boy, slipping a girl in there would have been a dead giveaway.

Afternoon: Counter Narcotics meeting. Slight Friday morning feel about the place – rather quiet.

Sunday

Combined GO (General Officer) level meeting with the Coalition and ourselves held in our Command Group dining facility – good meeting. ISAF and the Coalition have an excellent working relationship.

Before it started, Danny Van Laethem and I were standing outside in the fresh air chatting amid a crowd of assorted ISAF officers and soldiers, who were waiting to go into the adjacent main dining facility. A small party of US soldiers approached shooing everyone out of the way snapping, *"General Officer approaching, General Officer approaching"*. They walked right up to us and then from behind his Aviator shades Danny barked, *"I am a General Officer"*.

This caused some discombobulation. Calm was quickly restored by the distracting arrival of more US Generals in assorted huge 4x4s. All soldiers and officers must salute generals, so this results in the entire dinner queue and the escort party erupting in an out-break of salutes and genuflection.

Working session with some ISAF staff officers on PRT issues they can help with.

Dinner downtown Kabul with Phil Wilkinson in his nice house in a little guarded compound. We share a regimental background. After a successful career including deep Northern Ireland expertise, Phil had left the Army and ploughed an interesting furrow for himself. He had been a Senior Research Fellow at Kings College London's International Policy Institute developing the concept and practice of Security Sector Reform which we are now all up to our necks in. After a job in Iraq, he was now the Director of the UK's support to Afghanistan's Office of the National Security Council. Some of his Afghan colleagues from there join us. We discuss security and development generally and Disarming Illegal Armed Groups (DIAG) more specifically. We eat Afghan food and Phil and I have a glass of Lindeman's Shiraz.

Monday

Fly to the US Bagram Air Base with Lieutenant General Erdagi. It's about 40 miles north of Kabul in Parwan Province, south of the Hindu Kush – on the

Kabul side of that mountain wall. Serious agenda, but equally a bit of a 'Boys Own' day out.

Great helicopter flight - rather taxi-like ride at a few hundred meters altitude and a steady pace. We overfly a mix of mudbrick villages, interlinked walled farms, and stretches of arid landscape with a just a few Kuchi nomads tending goats and camels.

The farms are mostly in walled compounds with little walled orchards typically growing apricots, apples, and pears or sometimes almonds. Root crops like potatoes are grown too.

At Bagram, we get some great briefings and are driven round the base. Its immense scale says everything about American power projection. Fleets of assorted combat aircraft are parked up in rows:

> A10 'Tank Buster' aircraft
> EA6 Prowler Electronic Warfare aircraft
> AH64 Apache helicopter gunships
> CH47 Chinook heavy transport helicopters
> UH60 Blackhawk helicopters
> C12 Hurons – military executive aircraft
> C130s in a long Heathrow-like line-up.

Back at Kabul, in the evening the Command Group have a special dinner in the Turkish Embassy. It's in a very grand building located in a remarkable private estate of a garden with a beautiful swimming pool. Wonderful formal dinner hosted by the Ambassador.

Tuesday

Spend time working with UNAMA and National Security Council advisers to determine which province in ISAF's area will be used as a pilot province for DIAG.

The original Demobilization, Disarmament and Reintegration (DDR) programme for the major groups of combatants and their heavy weapons (tanks, artillery, air defence weapons) is ending. Japan was the G8 lead for that activity. DIAG is basically a successor programme to address lower tier warlords with mostly automatic rifles, machine guns, rockets, mines, and other nasties. Separating these out from groups of armed villagers or tribesmen will be tricky. Everyone in the countryside over twelve years old has an AK47 automatic rifle.

Some warlords are little tyrants. We do not know what weaponry they have. This makes it difficult to know if they have surrendered their arsenal or thrown us a bone.

In isolated areas we are told people won't know the difference between ISAF and the Soviets. We are all just armed *feringhees* (white foreigners) who shouldn't be there. So, if ISAF show-up, the locals are likely to grab their AK47s and have a pop. Complicated.

The people want it, politicians want it, and it

needs to happen. It will have an Afghan face. The National Directorate of Security will provide intelligence on the 1800 or so armed groups and the Afghan military and police will manage it on the ground. The approach will be dialogue based reinforced with community-based incentives. No heavy handed and likely fruitless searches. Encourage and cajole rather than coerce. ISAF is to be very much in the back seat.

Office call on Deputy Minister of Interior Shahmahmood Miakhel. He produces the Governor of Badakhshan who is clearly worried by some factional fighting that has broken out in the isolated north of the province.

Wednesday

Office call by Deputy Director UK Special Forces. Unconnected curry supper at Camp Souter with the visiting UK Chief of Defence Intelligence.

Thursday

PRT Executive Steering Committee Chaired by Deputy Minister Shahmahmood Miakhel and attended by other government ministers and all the Ambassadors whose countries contribute troops to PRTs. Some discussion of possible new PRTs.

Daikundi in Central Afghanistan is a bit of a front runner. It's a rocky wasteland. Even the Afghans round the table don't seem to know much about it. It's poverty stricken, has a relatively benign security environment, and is mostly populated by Hazaras.

Panjshir, north of Kabul, is another option. It was the heartland of Tajik resistance to the Soviet occupation. The possibility is mooted that for a PRT to be acceptable to the fiercely independent people there, it might have to be without a military component. Nobody is sure how that would work.

Zaranj, nestled against the Iranian border in the far Southwest makes it to the list. The people there are mostly Balochi. It is a focal point for illicit trafficking of all kinds. A carefully designed PRT could help intercept that. It is very isolated and surrounded by miles of desert. There is no populated hinterland that would derive the usual benefits from the presence of a PRT.

Back at the ranch. Office call by a posse of folks from the UK Foreign Office and Ministry of Defence. They are out here with General John McColl, PM Blair's Special Envoy to President Karzai. Impressive credentials, but I am not sure how many generals Karzai needs - he seems surrounded by them.

We learn of an accident. Two UK soldiers not seriously injured, five Afghan civilians so seriously they might die through the night. Much work to determine ground truth facts with a view to bringing Afghans into Kabul for better treatment.

Friday

Doctor's report indicates Afghan casualties not as serious as first thought.

Week Thirteen
(Kabul; Faisabad and Farah cancelled; Kandahar
and Baku airports; Home)

Saturday
Collect a visiting Brit Air Marshall from Kabul Airport.
Major General Wachter asked me to do this for him
while he is away and said I could use his close
protection detachment for the purpose.

I decide to take my own vehicle. On passing the
Headquarters building General Wachter's folks follow
on in two armoured black Mercedes G Class trucks. At
the airport it turns out there is some problem unloading
the luggage, so the Air Marshall and I set off in my
vehicle leaving the German team to kindly bring along
the luggage. We drive slowly through dense local traffic
chatting away to each other. After a time, we become
aware of a loud piercing siren behind us. Vehicles,

donkeys, and people begin rapidly pulling over to the side of the road in an immense crush. Thinking it is an emergency, we pull over too. We are overtaken by two black Mercedes G Class trucks with blue flashing lights and sirens blaring. The Air Marshall turns to me and says," *That will be my luggage then*".

Join Lieutenant General Erdagi for a meeting with Munshi Abdul Mahjid, the incoming Governor of Badakhshan. Rather impressive character with a huge white beard, no moustache, and a calm manner. We talk about illegal militias and poppy. He insists there is no poppy in Kishim in Badakhshan, which is where the eradication force thinks it is going next.

Attend Counter-Narcotics Working Group at the Ministry of Interior.

Later, we learn that a young woman has been stoned to death for alleged adultery in a village near Faisabad.

Sunday

Fly to Faisabad in a UK C130 with our vehicles on board. We cannot land as there is too much low cloud over the runway.

Recover lost afternoon by visiting UNAMA to discuss further which province in the ISAF area will be the pilot project for DIAG.

Monday

25th April. At dawn on this day in 1915 the Australian and New Zealand Army Corps (ANZACs) landed at Gallipoli in Turkey, as part of a British force (Turkey being on Germany's side in World War One).

A few years ago, I attended the 'ANZAC Dawn

Memorial Service' in Melbourne as a guest of the
Australian Army. We exited our hotel in Melbourne at
0345 hours and joined the thickening throng of citizens.
First a few hundred, then thousands, then tens of
thousands – the old, the young, babes in arms - until
there were 300,000 of us. There was a short service,
with buglers, and a moment of intense silence.

After the silence, veterans of more recent
conflicts gave their testimonials in the Melbourne dawn.
One old lady croaked into the microphone that in World
War Two she had been a nurse in a military field
hospital overrun by the Japanese. They forced all the
doctors, nurses and walking wounded down to the beach
and into the sea, where they machine gunned them.
Japanese officers walked amongst the floating corpses
shooting them in the head. She survived to bear witness.
'Lest We Forget', the horrors of war and the cruelty that
flows from unbridled nationalism and dehumanizing
hatred of every kind.

We are meant to fly to Farah today in the far
Southwest. Weather is against us and the trip is called
off at 0600.

Office day ensues in which I get on with all the
little things I want to crack before going on 'R&R' at the
end of the week. R&R is Rest and Recuperation leave
and in the British Army is usually for two weeks during
a six-month tour of active service. Long gone are the
days, for UK at least, when soldiers went to war and
came back when it was over.

R&R is tricky to manage in a fighting unit as a
great chunk of it is away on R&R at any one time and
that impacts effectiveness. Also, stuff happens while you
are away on R&R. In Kosovo, I came back from R&R

and discovered I had been given a different job for the rest of my tour there. Easy to talk about longer tours as some do, and about less or no R&R, if you are not the guy out there on the tour. There was this RAF guy in Belize who was the most miserable man alive. The RAF did four-month tours there and the Army six. He apparently on his arrival interview told the lovely Brigadier in command of our troops in Belize that there was no continuity in his role, and it ought to be a twelve-month tour. The Brig told him he was absolutely right, and that he could be the first. I think he was on suicide watch.

Much outrage over the stoning to death of the young woman, Amina, both here and in international press. Typically, in these killings, a well-like pit is dug to about shoulder or head height. The woman is usually bound in her burqa and placed upright in the pit. A crowd of men then throw stones, or really rocks at her until she dies of blunt trauma injury. Badakhshan Chief of Police is on the case. Reportedly her male relatives took part and her mother approved.

Evening: Gallipoli Dinner at Camp Souter caused by Colonel James Denny, the Fusilier-in-Chief of Afghanistan. Lancashire, Munster, Dublin, and Inniskilling Fusiliers had all fought there. The Lancashire Fusiliers won six Victoria Crosses before breakfast on that fateful day.

Outstanding effort by James and his gang. Chefs revel in a chance to show off. We have Chicken and Roast Red Pepper Roulade, Rack of Lamb, and steamed Chocolate Pudding Ganache. A small squad of Gurkha pipers march in to round off the evening with a hair-raising rendition of Highland Cathedral.

The little menu prominently displays the famous quote by Kemal Ataturk, the founding father of modern Turkey, which is chiseled into the Gallipoli memorial there *"......You mothers who sent their sons from far away countries wipe away your tears. Your sons are now lying in our bosom and are in peace. After having lost their lives on this land they have become our sons as well"*.

The invited Turkish Generals and General Wachter totally love it. Tremendous craic. I did not know it then, but my next Gallipoli Dinner would be in Baghdad.

Tuesday

Hosted a PRT Development Officers' meeting for DfID/USAID equivalents. Robert did a great job pulling it all together. Much angst and absurd sensitivity from some embassies, but it all goes swimmingly well. Netherlands Ambassador, Martin de La Bey, joined us and was extremely supportive. A good morning in the trenches.

One of the German civilians had been to the village in the Urgu district where the stoning occurred. He gave the village elders in the local Shura (council) a piece of his mind. They all sat there with their heads bowed like naughty schoolboys who knew they shouldn't have let it happen. That sort of thing isn't in anybody's job description. Many would be quick to say it was an Afghan matter and hide behind that. But I think it was a pretty ballsy thing to do - going there alone and saying what needed to be said, as a representative of humanity.

Strange how cowardice invariably goes hand in

hand with acts of vile abuse. There is something universal in that. The stoning and killing of the beautiful widow for sleeping with the Alan Bates character, Basil, in *Zorba the Greek* is a grim depiction of the same mob mindset and the hand in glove cowardice to let it happen. People, including Basil, knew what was happening was wrong but failed to speak out, let alone intervene, even as the deed unfolded before their eyes.

Lots of gloomy intelligence reports about suicide bombers and much else. Lead Counter Narcotics Working Group meeting in the headquarters and attend routine operations update.

Wednesday

Attend Counter Narcotics meeting in Ministry of Interior chaired by General Doud. We discuss reviewing eradication strategy.

Lunch with NATO Military Committee – a bunch of Three-Star General Officers who are assigned to NATO Headquarters in Brussels.

Some are represented on this trip by their One-Star deputies. This happily includes for UK, Brigadier Will Cook who was my boss in a previous existence. He was a hard task master but was always fair and good company. He had been especially helpful to me as I went off to Kosovo on promotion to Brigadier.

Italy is represented by Brigadier General Paolo Terzano with whom I had enjoyed a happy year's service in Kosovo. It had been an Italian led headquarters under the fabulous and volcanic General Fabio Mini. The habit of many Italian officers there was to adjourn after lunch to a little bar in the headquarters for an espresso and a cigarette - I sometimes joined for the craic.

Afternoon: press on with deck clearing prior to leave. I feel chipper about progress from my perspective at this point.

The PRT Handbook is well received and hosted on the NATO IT system. PRTs report finding it extremely useful.

PRTs now report against 'Measures of Effectiveness' based on the 'Province Assessment Model' in the PRT Handbook. This should enable an objective assessment of progress across ISAF.

I increasingly see NATO's expansion around Afghanistan as a risk to success due to its leaden decision making, fragmented effort, and overly military-centric approach. Also, any viable exit strategy must be based on both an effective Afghan National Army *and* an effective Afghan National Police. Something NATO as an institution does not seem to get.

Afghanistan for its part seems highly atomized. Villages are impossibly far from even district and provincial centers, let alone Kabul which is on another planet. Sometimes I think of Macondo, the imaginary isolated Columbian village in Gabriel Garcia Marquez's *'One Hundred Years of Solitude'*. Macondo becomes increasingly connected to the outside world bringing many benefits but also, over time, change, estrangement, tensions, and conflict, resulting ultimately in dissolution and depopulation. Rather like the Highlands of Scotland or Western Ireland. One wonders too if anyone in London, Edinburgh or Dublin really cared much about those wild backwaters.

Office call by some Danish researchers.

Evening BBQ for the Military Committee. Pack.

Thursday

Big pow wow with the staff to get them working on a whole range of things that need doing while I am away. They are keen to help. For the majority, English is a second language. They are expected to be literate and conduct professional conversations. Try finding British officers who could do that in French or German never mind in Turkish or something.

One morning when Charles Comyn was away, we were going through the diary that he produces. The Commander looks up and says, *"What is this N.B?"* Lots of blank stares so I chip in, *"Nota Bene sir, it's Latin for note well"*. He looks around the room slowly with a big smile and says, *"My goodness, here we all are in this multi-national headquarters in Afghanistan, struggling every day to work in English, and my Military Assistant wants us all to learn Latin."*

Finish packing. Clear decks.

Formal dinner with NATO Military Committee in the main dining facility. Great craic with Will and Paolo. Seems unreal that we should be dining together in Kabul – one for the scrap book.

Friday

R&R begins. I have now been in Kabul for exactly three months. I realize that I have not been carpet shopping. This needs to be a priority for the second half of the tour.

Fly from Kabul on one of these huge C17s to Kandahar. It has a cargo from UK of 500-pound bombs (quarter of a metric ton) and various other ordnance destined for our Harriers in Kandahar, Kabul being the first in-country stop. Spend an hour or so on the ground at Kandahar in sweltering heat before being loaded back onto the plane, just in time for the smoke alarm to go off. This necessitated an evacuation drill. Further ninety minutes hanging around on the tarmac runway with its melting frying pan surface and no shade. Fire service guys finally sort out the smoke alarms.

C17

I sit up in the cockpit for the next leg of the flight to Baku in Azerbaijan. As we approach Baku airport something spoofs the Defensive Aids Suite on the aircraft causing the flares to discharge. This requires paperwork and rectifying in Baku. Another long delay hanging about. Seems endless to be honest. I am reminded of a bad attitude Sergeant Major I once had, who said *"I've been in the army for twenty-two years sir, and I've spent nineteen of them hanging about"*.

Arrive home in the wee hours of Saturday.

Weeks Fourteen and Fifteen
(R&R and While I Was Away)

Wonderful two weeks at home. Great to be together as a family. Over too quickly. Depart UK on Sunday 15 May.

   While I was away there was widespread rioting across Afghanistan in which seventeen people were killed. Sparked by protests at reported desecration of the Quran in Guantanamo Bay. This was part of a wave of protests across the Moslem world. A further fifteen died in demonstrations in Egypt, Indonesia, Palestine, Pakistan, and Sudan.

   In Kabul there was a suicide bombing at an internet café killing four people, plus two rocket attacks, an attempted kidnapping, and then a successful kidnapping of an Italian lady.

   Three Afghan women were raped and hanged in Zaman Zhil village about five kilometers from Pol-e Khumri. They were then dumped by the roadside. One had a sign round her neck saying not to work for foreign aid agencies. One of the women worked for a Bangladeshi charity that sought to help widows through micro-credit, another was a local civil servant, and the third is unidentified. A hitherto unknown group called Junbish Jawanan Islam (Islamic Youth Convention) claimed responsibility.

In another village near Pol-e Khumri, an arms cache exploded at the home of a supposedly disarmed warlord, killing many local people.

There was an exchange of gun fire between Afghan police and the Afghan National Army in Herat.

In Faryab Province there was a gun battle between rival warlords in the Shirin Tagab district, about forty-five kilometers north of Maimana.

Week Sixteen
(Pol-e Khumri, Herat and Kandahar)

Monday

Landed at 1020 AM local after a smooth overnight flight sitting up with the pilots on a C17. Went straight to work. Everyone is consumed with the ongoing kidnapping of the Italian lady, Ms Clemintina Cantoni, and the continuing stand-off between rival factions in Shirin Tagab.

The Herat shooting came and went but there are lessons to learn. Afghan police say the killing of the women near Pol-e Khumri has many motives and is unconnected to the presence of the PRT.

Tuesday

Fly with Lieutenant General Erdagi to Pol-e Khumri PRT via Konduz. We transfer in Konduz from a C130 aircraft into German CH-53G helicopters. This is starting to feel like catching buses. We literally walk off one and onto the other.

We then fly to Pol-e Khrumri, as before, at a height of 5 meters or so and a speed of 140 knots (over 200 kph). We veer down some tight valleys. Impressive pilot skills, but we scatter livestock again. The flight profile mitigates surface to air missile threats but puts them in AK47 rifle or rocket propelled grenade range and no doubt stokes resentment.

We have a good visit to the PRT and discuss many issues including the killing of the three women.

Return in time for the evening operations update and dinner downtown with Phil Wilkinson and the National Security Council folks.

Wednesday

Fly to Herat in a C130 with General Back. He is in good form today. Bumpy landing. The plane is all over the place.

We attend an unexceptional 'Change of

Command' ceremony at the Herat Forward Support Base by the airport. It marks transfer of authority for this support function from the Italians to the Spanish. The Spanish have done a great job setting up the FSB, helped by the US providing forty C17 flights.

We then drive to the PRT in the city. I am again struck by Herat. It bristles modern buildings, and the roads are great. The city doesn't look like it needs much help from a reconstruction perspective, but it has security issues below the surface.

We get a standard briefing at the PRT. The shoot-out between the Afghan Army and Police in Herat is discussed. It was a short-lived and rather weird incident. Everyone now understands the need to reach out behind the scenes early to calm matters and initiate dialogue. PRTs should not take sides in disputes between factions, but they should support legitimate authority (whenever it is clear who that is) and try to calm things down.

Uneventful return trip flying once again across Afghanistan's mountainous expanse and then driving through the mayhem that is Kabul.

Taliban kill eleven Afghans working on a US funded 'Alternative Livelihoods' project in Helmand province.

Shaima Rezayee, aged twenty-four, a host on an MTV-style music show in Afghanistan, is shot in the head and killed at her home in Kabul.

Thursday

Learn today that NATO does not want my role and a dedicated PRT office to continue into the Italian rotation. This is frustrating. I also learn today that UK want me out a month early to begin a new job in London and have no plans to replace me. I now need to dissipate my knowledge across the headquarters and accelerate documenting the more directive approach to PRTs.

Office call by the Commanding Officer of 22 SAS. We sit with Robert in the sunshine in the headquarters garden and have a wide-ranging chat over cold drinks.

Get interviewed by the BBC and local TV and radio. A laugh despite the gravity of the issues discussed. Perhaps my local TV interview will be beamed into some of those satellite dishes around the country.

At the routine Command Group dinner, the Commander informs everybody of my early departure. Nazim is extremely disappointed. Suleyman says I can't possibly go early as I am '*Potts Pasha*' now. Being fully integrated with my Turkish friends I must complete the tour and return with them to Istanbul. This causes much amusement and lightens the moment. Suleyman is also very insistent that it is *Potts Pasha*, not *Pasha Potts*.

The Commander says we should all come to Istanbul for a party at the end of the tour. Wonderful idea.

Friday

Fly to Kandahar with General Back – great trip.

My dad followed his elder brother into the Merchant Navy. When he came home on leave after long absences, he would take me to see kitsch movies about the Northwest Frontier and the like. Stuffed full of colonial stereotypes no doubt, but nobody noticed that back then. *The Brigand of Kandahar* stuck in my mind with its big screen cavalry charges and dusky maidens as my dad called them.

Our visit disappointingly doesn't take us into the city. It has a population of over 300,000, mainly Pashtuns and it is famous for its bustling bazaars. Ahmad Shah Durrani, of the Durrani Pashtun tribal group, founded the modern Kingdom of Afghanistan in the mid Eighteenth Century and laid out the city. His mausoleum is here. Adjacent to it is the Shrine of the Cloak of the Prophet Mohammad, which houses said holy relic. Last seen in public draped over the Taliban leader Mullah Omar who did a few twirls in it to rally his troops and confer legitimacy on his leadership.

We are briefed in the Coalition Regional Headquarters 'South'. It has a fight on its hands, especially in Kandahar province. A serious hot spot is Spin Boldak on the border with Pakistan about sixty kilometers from Kandahar. It is halfway between Kandahar and Quetta in Pakistan, where the Taliban leadership enjoy safe haven. Quetta rather weirdly is also where the Pakistan Army Staff College is located, and UK traditionally sends two officers there every year.

Pakistan also hosts Taliban bases and is permissive of its recruiting and training efforts. It's impossible to win a fight if the rules are that you must stay in the boxing ring, while the other fellow can land a punch when you are not looking, then hop out of the ring and wave two fingers from the safety of the crowd.

Great swathes of territory over the border in Pakistan have been run by the Pathan tribes themselves since the days of British India. When I was first commissioned, I was produced with the rest of the new batch of officers at a huge regimental cocktail party. One of the many guests was a long-retired major who like many others there was equipped with ruddy cheeks, a charcoal suit and a Gin and Tonic which he gripped in his fist. Most of us would soon be posted off to Germany, which he thought would be a colossal bore. He regaled us all with stories of when he was at our stage of life in the 1930s, fighting Pathan tribesmen on the Northwest Frontier. Made it all sound like tremendous sport. I thought at the time that it sounded more like something out of the Nineteenth Century than the Twentieth, and now here we all are, in the Twenty-First.

Nowadays the Taliban areas over there are a magnet for other Jihadists. It's a spawn centre for terrorists and a threat to the world, not just the venue for a local brawl.

Denying this safe haven militarily is well beyond the scope of ISAF, and indeed the Coalition. Likely needs a broad-based international effort in support of the Pakistan government, who need to be energized to do something. Can't imagine anyone is up for that right now. It's a mess that threatens to unstitch our best efforts here.

The US commander says if he could have another PRT in the south of the country he would have a second one in Kandahar. Useful to know. He also says dust storms cause a no-fly 120 days per year.

We then have an airfield tour. See Predator Unmanned Aerial Vehicle and have a demo of its impressive capabilities. The US have had versions of it for a decade now, so I am familiar with it.

Predator at Kandahar

They can fly for about twenty-two hours. Once launched by the ground crew of contractors in Kandahar, the mission is controlled via satellite from Nellis Airforce base in Nevada, USA. They can carry Hellfire missiles. We watch a recording of a Hellfire attack on some armed Taliban popping in and out of a wee house. The missile was fired by an operator in Nellis, who probably went and had a Big Mac afterwards or met their mates in a bowling alley, while the aftermath unfolded thousands of miles away.

For those on the receiving end of the Hellfire missile it would be like a thunderbolt. The Pashtun social code, Pashtunwali, seems based on honour, hospitality, misogyny, and vengeance. So, if those killed turn out not to be Taliban, their male relatives, potentially in a large extended family, will feel obliged to join the Taliban to avenge them. Even these so called 'precision' air strikes risk becoming a 'Recruiting Sergeant' for the Taliban unless they can just hit the bad guys every time – a tall order, mission impossible really.

The alternative of course is to fight these people on their own terms – man to man. Why would anyone want to do that? John Masters said of Pathans, in *Bugles and a Tiger*, '*these fierce men, physically the hardest people on earth ... they use sharp stones for toilet paper....a Pathan walks with the grace of a man eating tiger*'.

The terrain and weather are amongst the most severe on the planet, which limits the scope for air strikes anyhow. It all feels a bit grim and far removed from Kabul and the North.

In the evening, back in Kabul, we have a Norwegian Constitution Day dinner. Magnificent sea food buffet absolutely groaning with lobster. The Norwegians seem to regard this giant crustacean as normal fayre in the way the Brits would Cod, or Plaice. All laid on by Colonel Roar Lagerud, our wonderful mustachioed Viking.

Week Seventeen
(Kabul, Pol-e Khumri, Konduz and Farah)

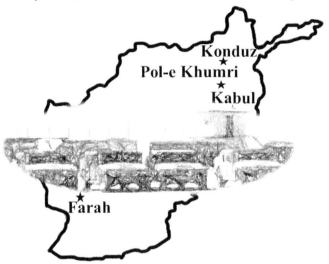

Saturday

Office day. David Armitage calls by with Huw Lawford to discuss Information Operations in support of Counter Narcotics.

Sunday

Fly to Pol-e Khumri via Konduz again. Change once more from a C130 to a CH-53G at Konduz for another 5 meter-high, 140 knots ride to Pol-e Khumri.

CH-53G at Pol-e Khumri

After a good visit, I return to Konduz again in the waiting CH-53G helicopter. At Konduz I transfer into a C160 aircraft. Weather has closed in. We take off anyway. It only has twin engines and can't get over the Hindu Kush in the worsening weather. It turns around and comes back to Konduz, dropping off the passengers to spend the night. The C160 bumbles on to Termez.

The Germans pick up everyone from the airport and run us all into the Konduz PRT. It has plenty of spare accommodation, but it is pretty spartan. Luckily, I always travel with a packed rucksack – sleeping bag, bivvy bag, washing and shaving gear, flak jacket and helmet.

Good evening in Konduz. Convivial and useful conversation over dinner with civil and military leadership. Some of the guys from Badakhshan are there too.

Monday

Drive out of the Konduz PRT to the airfield and return to Kabul via Mazar-e-Sharif in a Turkish C130.

Tuesday

PRT Conference and BBQ – huge success. Lieutenant General Erdagi praises the Maimana PRT for mediating a ceasefire after the shoot-out at Shirin Tagab. Nobody expects anyone in a PRT to interpose themselves between factions in a fire fight. It is more about knowing who the various actors are and initiating constructive dialogue. ISAF can support by influencing the local factions' patrons in Kabul.

Wednesday

Fortnightly Counter Narcotics meeting in Minister Doud's office. Have good discussions with folks from the United Nations Office on Drugs and Crime (UNODC).

Thursday

Fly to Farah in Southwest Afghanistan via Shindand. Party includes Lieutenant General Erdagi, Major General Kamiya (US) from the Coalition Force, and Kamiya's wonderful Political Advisor, Robert Maggi (aka Turk), who organized it all. Lieutenant Colonel Andy Santa-Pinter, the Farah PRT commander, has hitched a lift with us after being stranded at the PRT conference due to adverse weather.

Militarily, Farah is in the Coalition's 'West' region so it will shortly transfer to ISAF. Hence the trip.

We fly from Kabul in two swanky C12 Huron executive aircraft - plush interior with leather seats. Great view of Kabul as we fly over it. The Hindu Kush looks wonderful with bright sunshine, snow, and clouds.

The landscape becomes more barren as we approach Shindand. There we transfer in searing heat from the C12s into two UH60 Blackhawk helicopters. They flew up from Kandahar solely for the purpose of flying us to Farah.

Switching at Shindand

The Blackhawk flight from Shindand to Farah takes an hour. We fly straight and fast at a few hundred meters altitude. The door gunner mans an M60D machine gun, unloaded but with an ammo belt to hand. During the entire flight, we see nothing but a barren expanse of rocks.

At one point we fly over the freshly laid asphalt strip that is Highway 01, the so-called 'Ring Road'. This is the 1,400-mile (2,200-kilometer) two lane loop that will connect Afghanistan's major cities. It has existed partially for years in various forms and degrees of completeness. Stretches are being laid anew or refurbished to fully connect all the way around Afghanistan. There is nothing in any direction on either side of it. It is empty too and runs to the horizon like a pencil line on a blank sheet of paper.

We land at the PRT. It is well organized, and we get briefings and a show round. They operate on the standard US format of the Department of State and USAID working hand in glove with the military, who here are mostly Rangers.

The place has a Wild West feel about it. They have mortars in their 'defense section'. These are like small artillery pieces that can lob explosive shells about eight kilometers. A step change in security profile from the PRTs in the North.

HMMWV (Humvee)

120mm Mortar

We are told an Afghan National Army (ANA) Battalion 'a Kandak' will soon be based in the area. There are local police in Farah town who have divided into opposing factions, but no Afghan National Police yet. There is also a National Directorate of Security section in town – a sort of Afghan MI5/FBI.

On taking off, we circle over the town before heading out across the desert again. Utterly barren and uninhabited, bar some Kuchi nomads. We cross the Ring Road again and can see along it for miles and miles, this time there are a couple of trucks on it. We switch at Shindand once more and luxuriate in the C12 flight back to Kabul. A great trip.

We learn on return that at about 0900 hours this morning a vehicle from the Pol-e Khumri PRT was damaged by a small explosion. It was moving in a six-vehicle convoy. Two soldiers slightly hurt. We do not yet know if this is a deliberate attack, unexploded ordnance or what.

Friday

Chilled day – first chance to play catch-up since getting back.

I go along to a sort of Friday market in the ISAF camp, just inside the security perimeter. Lots of stalls selling all kinds of artefacts, but many of the sellers are aggressive and grabby. Knives with beautiful handles of blue Lapis Lazuli mined in Badakhshan seem popular. I buy two fine Buzkashi whips.

They are about 30 inches long. Just under half the length is a leather core with rawhide braided over it. The rest is a wood handle decorated with silver-coloured metal strips bound round it to give the impression of it being silver – which of course the guy on the stall insists it is. They look grand and will match a pair of slightly more rustic ones I picked up in Kazakhstan last year.

In the 19th Century 'hordes' of nomadic peoples still roamed the Central Asian steppes on horseback. The Russian Empire was the agent of their destruction. The building of railroads, the coming of towns, and enforced boarding schools for their children erased their way of life. Sovietization finally did for them. Firstly, in the 1920s with industrialization, mineral exploitation, female emancipation, and forced settlement. Then in the 1930s, the 'collective ownership' of agricultural produce and livestock destroyed the patriarchal social structure and resulted in starvation and death of people and animals on a Biblical scale. State-building Soviet style.

Evening: Command Group BBQ at Kabul International Airport. After that we all go out onto the runway to see the Turkish construction company there resurfacing it by night. My kids would have loved it. Dozens of huge machines and hundreds of men working away under great clusters of bright lights fitted on wheeled towers. They are laying a polymer coat on the runway and making asphalt, then laying it. It would take sixty nights to do the job bit by bit, leaving the runway operable during the day. The cost we were told was 13.5M USD. All the machines had been brought overland from Turkey, through Iran.

Week Eighteen
(Kabul and Herat)

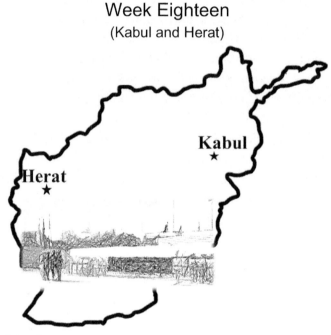

Saturday

Send routine update to my chain of command in UK summarizing progress and making a few recommendations.

Go over to the US Coalition Headquarters to help brief Counter Narcotics to their newly arrived commander, Lieutenant General Carl Eikenberry.

Later, the Director of Iceland's Crisis Response Unit calls by to discuss Iceland increasing its contribution to the PRTs. Turns out it is my old roommate from Maimana.

Sunday

Another office day. I write a PRT strategy. Nothing dramatic – just building toward the already agreed 'end state' of not being needed and offering various ways to get there.

None of the Afghans I meet in the bazaars complain about the Taliban, warlords, or narcotics – our security concerns. They all want basic medical care, clean water, food in the market, and schools for their children. They are vexed by corruption and by remote and ineffective officialdom. These aren't military issues.

Monday

01:18 hours: a 107 mm rocket, not usually found in the Guy Fawkes collection, is fired in the general direction of our camp from a range of about eight kilometers. It impacts the Chief Engineer's Corimec cabin, eighty feet or so from mine, and explodes. Mercifully, he is not in it and nobody is hurt.

The woosh and the noise wakes everyone. Having been the father of three children under seventeen months old, I sleep through it. It is only when the siren goes off that I awake and throw my clothes on. Rest of night passed in the Joint Operations Centre monitoring events and drinking tea.

Guys on the operations team think the incident is a result of the withdrawal of the Apache helicopters who did overflight patrols of possible rocket launch sites. Short of interviewing the culprits we will never know that for sure.

At about 0930 a bicycle bomb goes off in Kabul. The target is one of our vehicles, but an Afghan taxi overtakes it on the inside at the critical moment and gets the full force of the blast. All five passengers in the taxi are injured badly.

Drive over to Camp Souter to have a British

lunch, check on what's going on from a UK perspective, cash a cheque, and catch up with the Brits.

Tuesday

Rioting at Takhar – reportedly three killed. We scramble two F-16 fighter jets to fly low over the crowd and five CH-53G helicopters to buzz the area. We send two C130 aircraft to Mazar-e-Sharif to pick up the UK Quick Reaction Force company. Crowd disperses – big success. Huge overkill, but good to see the system can work.

Fly to Herat for the 'Change of Command' ceremony to mark the handover of security assistance responsibilities in Western Afghanistan from the US-led Coalition to NATO. The Italians will be the lead nation there drawing together the efforts of Spanish, Lithuanians, and US troops including the Farah PRT.

I am just here to spectate. I have never got on very well with parades, having been blessed with two left feet and uncoordinated arms. At Sandhurst, I once committed the capital offence of dropping my bayonet on parade. The Irish Guards Sergeant Major bellowed across the square, *"Mister Potts sir, your head is full of potato bread"*.

The food laid on afterwards by the Italians is astonishing in scale and quality. It includes a whole Parmesan to scoop lumps out of. The heat is unbearable. Journey back to the airport in a sweltering bus with no air conditioning is just awful. This is followed by long overcrowded C130 flight to Kabul.

Can't help wondering how relations with the Iranians will play out there. They are doubtless unamused to be surrounded on three sides by American forces: in Afghanistan, the Persian Gulf and Iraq. Equally there is no love lost between them and the Taliban who once seized the Iranian Consulate in Mazar-e-Sharif and executed the Consul. They are concerned for their Hazara Shi'ite co-religionists and have legitimate cultural and commercial influence in Western Afghanistan. They probably prefer a stable Afghanistan but will not want ISAF to have an easy ride.

Evening: dinner at the Turkish Embassy hosted by Ambassador, Bulent Tulun. He is a wonderful host, and the Embassy's attractive grounds are an oasis. The main guests are Ambassador Antonio Maria Costa of the UNODC and his team, the Italian Ambassador Snr Ettore Francesco Sequi, and the British Embassy Drugs Team leader. They wanted to discuss increased ISAF support to Counter Narcotics, especially through the PRTs. I am sat centre table and cross-examined as an expert witness.

Afghan Special Narcotics Force attacked Bahram Shah today - a large heavily guarded drugs bazaar in Southern Helmand that straddles the border with Pakistan. Huge coup. Baddies run away, 2.5 metric tonnes of opium and 250 kilograms of heroin destroyed plus a large quantity of precursor chemicals used in the heroin production process. No casualties.

Wednesday

Suicide bomb in a Kandahar mosque kills twenty.

Thursday

Quiet and slow day. Have coffee in the Headquarters Garden with Danny Van Laethem,

Commander of the Air Task Force. He retires from the Belgian Forces on return and might be taking up a job flying DC10 cargo planes around Africa. Sounds great.

The German PRTs' civilian leaders call by. They are down on some embassy business and have a gap in their schedule, so they drop into the office. Good to see them and we have a great conversation.

Evening: reception in the garden of the Italian Embassy. All the politicos are there. Still no news on the kidnapped Ms Cantoni. Soft drinks all around.

Friday

Go to gym as I usually do every day. As they say on active operations, *"there is nothing to do, except work and workout"*. Fighting fit - down to 12st 02 lbs (77KG).

Week Nineteen
(Kabul, Bamiyan, historic Herat and Qala-e-Naw)

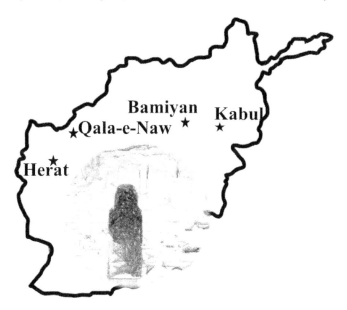

Saturday

Attended Finnish Armed-Forces' Day bash in a barracks somewhere across Kabul. Astonishing seafood buffet. More lobster.

Sunday

Office day. My mother always said, "*Nobody lies on their deathbed wishing they'd spent more time in the office*".

Monday

Another office day.

Plans to close PRT Office on 30th June are

formalized and issued.

Good chat in the garden with Ambassador Mikko Pyhala the Finnish Ambassador to 'Asia and Oceania'. It struck me that he has enviable scope for trips.

Can't complain though, I've had plenty of great trips. In one job I had so many trips I joked that I worked for the office of military tourism. I did a lot of scuba diving on the Great Barrier Reef off the back of some. On a trip to Hawaii, after flying to the other side of the world, I arrived in my hotel room on a Saturday night in time for the kickoff of the England Brazil World Cup match. Over a cold beer I flicked through the Yellow Pages for a dive operation that could take me next morning. Sure enough, at the appointed time a gigantic black four-wheel drive pulled up outside the hotel. The guy driving looked like something out of a heavy metal band and his partner was a Baywatch Babe. Off we went. Great dive buddies.

Evening: dinner hosted by Minister Cetin for the visiting NATO Deputy Secretary General, Alessandro Minuto Rizzo and a posse of visiting NATO Ambassadors. Other invitees included Ambassadors from NATO countries accredited here in Kabul; and Jean Arnault the UN Special Representative of the Secretary General to Afghanistan, Francesco Vendrell the Special Representative of the EU, Karl Harbo the Head of the European Commission Delegation, Lieutenant General Karl Eikenberry the new Coalition commander, and our ISAF Command Group. It was held in the canteen, reconfigured into long tables.

Tuesday

Present ISAF medals on a little parade – mostly to Turkish soldiers in the headquarters. They are immensely proud. I pose for an individual photo with each of them.

Evening BBQ for a visiting Belgian General.

Wednesday

It's my birthday today.

Fly to Bamiyan with the two Deputy Commanders - Major Generals Herman Wachter and Reha Taskesen. Danny Van Laethem comes too. My purpose is to give everyone a shared understanding of what 'good can look like' in PRT terms.

Great boys' day out. Fly there in a Belgian C130. The engaging and pretty young woman pilot has spent six years flying F-16 fast jets.

Major General Wachter receives the traditional Kiwi Hakka welcome. He absolutely loves it.

We get a great briefing and show round which does the trick of impressing and enlightening everyone. The Kiwis are a perfect choice of exemplar: hugely impressive and neither American nor European.

After the briefing, the Kiwis give us morning tea and drive us out to the Buddhas for the inevitable touristic moment.

We chat to some UNESCO people who explain

that just throwing up concrete Buddha replacements would not be consistent with its status as a World Heritage Site. They say the destruction itself is part of what the site now is.

After the visit, as we take off, the plane banks slightly, framing the pilot's blonde ponytail in the cockpit window through which one can see below two Afghan women shuffling along in their burqas.

Back in Kabul I have a meeting in the garden with the PRT civilian leaders from Faisabad and Pol-e Khumri. After a good catchup we all go into my office to say farewell to my PA and to welcome her successor. The team have done an impromptu birthday party with bubbly, hot toad-in-the-hole (mashed potato and sausages), and a birthday cake. Great craic.

Thursday

Fly to Herat for an update on developments there and to see the new Spanish PRT at Qala-e-Naw. Charles Comyn comes along for the ride.

We are routed via 'milk-run' touchdowns in

Mazar-e-Sharif and Maimana. Passing over the Hindu Kush we see the usual stunning vista of snow-capped mountains, even in June, and vivid blue sky. Some clouds threaten in the distance.

We have a seriously long afternoon of briefings and discussions in a hot meeting room where lazy fans stir stifling air. We cover every aspect of the Region Headquarters, the support base and the PRT. We also talk to representatives from some civilian aid agencies.

We then go out in the cool of the evening to see Herat. Giuseppe hosts us with cheerful enthusiasm. We travel in his squad of black armoured four-wheel drives with his excellent black-clad, and well-armed, Carabinieri protection team.

Herat has experienced Alexander the Great, Genghis Khan, Tamerlane, and Babur, and was scarred by the British and the Soviets. It oozes history.

The 'Friday Mosque' is a magnificent first stop in the early evening light. It is a 15th Century creation of the Timurid dynasty – successors of Tamerlane the havoc-wreaking Tartar warlord. He stormed out of Central Asia and terrorized peoples from India to the fringes of Europe, capturing Herat in 1383. After his death in 1405 there was a period of internecine warfare from which his youngest son, Shah Rukh, emerged triumphant. He moved the Timurid capital from Samarkand in modern Uzbekistan to Herat. He and his Queen Gawhr Shad then inspired a cultural renaissance that merged influences of Central Asia and Persia. They built the mosque and much else besides. UNESCO have rehabilitated the local tile factory and restored the tile work. It looks stunning in the now soft light.

Next, a wonderful glass and artifact shop at which Charles buys some traditional blue glasses and decanters. An astonishing collection of old swords, muskets, and pistols catches my eye.

Giuseppe then takes us to his favourite carpet shop. The young merchant, Obdullah, sells me a beautiful reddish lamb's wool Bukhara style carpet from

Konduz and a soft brown camel hair carpet made by local Turkmen people, also in the Bukhara style.

After the carpet shopping, we go literally next door to a caravanserai. It is one of many in Herat. Camel trains sometimes had hundreds of heavily laden animals. They would have stopped here on their way along a branch of the network of Silk Routes from China and India to the Levant and back – a trade route plied over many centuries. This caravanserai is used today as a venue to wash and dry carpets.

From the roof top we look out over Herat. Calls to prayer fill the air. We have a wonderful view of the massive and impressive Citadel on the site of which a fortress has stood since the time of Alexander the Great. He came through here in 330 BCE (Before Common Era, BC in old speak). We can also see the five remaining fifty-five-meter-tall minarets of the Fifteenth Century Musalla complex beyond.

In the evening we return to the PRT. Giuseppe
and Aldo host us to a sumptuous al fresco supper. We
learn that Ms Cantoni has been released by the gangsters
who kidnapped her. We toast her health with a fine
Rioja.

Friday

We fly in two Spanish Cougar helicopters to
Qala-e-Naw, the capital of Baghdis province and about
130 kilometers Northeast of Herat. Giuseppe and Aldo
come too. Initially we fly over Herat city. Looking
down, we can see busy main roads and many modern
buildings that look like warehouses, small factories, or a
light industrial estate. There are a lot of green trees
interspersed amongst the buildings or in lines along the
roadsides and many simple mudbrick dwellings typical
of the villages too. The overall impression is of a
bustling city that could be almost anywhere.

We are soon crossing a very arid landscape in
bright morning sunshine. This monotonous vista seems
to last a long time. After an hour or so, villages appear
below, and the surrounding land looks more fertile.
Trees bearing pistachio grow on some of the rolling
hills. As we arrive at Qala-e-Naw we circle over the
little town. We hover whilst goats and children are
cleared from our landing site - a dirt runway littered by
the carcass of an abandoned civilian jet.

Qala-e-Naw is dirt poor. A river flows through

the town. We splash through a ford and up to the PRT.

Qala-e-Naw

Colonel Veiga, the Spanish Commander, shows us around. His Spanish soldiers and local workers have done a great job of construction and fitting-out in the two short weeks they have been here. They are now in the process of scoping out local relationships. Baghdis province is quite an isolated and odd place. Last year five Medicine sans Frontier workers were shot to death here in their clearly marked truck, causing MSF to withdraw from Afghanistan. Who would do that?

The Spanish have quite a few women in the PRT who are attracting great interest given all the local women are in burqas. We learn that female primary school enrolment in Baghdis province is only 1%. That means 99 in every 100 girls do not go to primary school. In early teens they pop on their burqas and at a young age are given in marriage, often to a much older man. Pregnancy often soon follows. There are cultural and economic reasons why families engage in this custom and practice, but as we learned previously it sometimes drives girls to pitiful acts of self-immolation.

Lack of access to education for girls leads to a shortage of nurses and midwives, let alone female obstetricians etc, so a cycle of appallingly high maternal mortality (death related to pregnancy and childbirth) and other ills continues. My Commander's mantra to the Afghans of *"educate your daughters"* is spot-on and as a father of a daughter I applaud it.

But what happens when a girl here learns to read – what is available to her to read, can her dad read, how does that work? In '*Out of Africa*' the village chief gives off at Karen Blixen for teaching children to read. He takes a machete and slashes a post making a deep mark just over a meter from the ground. Her interpreter explains *"The chief says children higher than this (mark) must not learn to read…. It is not good for tall people to know more than this chief. When these totos (below the mark) are tall, then this chief can be dead"*.

After a tour round the simple camp, we walkabout in Qala-e-Naw bazaar. Everyone is friendly and welcoming. Droves of men are walking to Friday prayers. Vendors dotted about sell fresh vegetables and wonderful heaps of potatoes in open topped white sacks or piled on great wicker trays. Tin pans and pots are stacked high, and kettles hang in great bunches. A man sells blocks of salt from a large box.

Droves of curious children run about laughing and giving us a thumbs up sign – hope it means the same thing here. Many children help on the stalls and some are left in sole charge.

The air is filled with the smells of fresh bread, burning charcoal and sizzling meat on little barbeques.

Later we visit the small US Embedded Training Team in the local Afghan National Army (ANA) contingent. These boys from small towns in the USA will spend a whole year or more in Qala-e-Naw living cheek by jowl with their Afghan comrades. They exude positivity and commitment to what needs to be done here if we are ever to go home leaving Afghan forces behind that can look after their country. I am not aware of any other nation yet providing ETTs in the ANA. It is the sort of thing UK is traditionally good at.

We leave Qala-e-Naw as we arrived, in the Cougars that had waited patiently on the airstrip.

Cougar
at Qala-e-Naw

This time on return we fly over a nomad encampment. Most of Afghanistan's 1.5 million nomads are Kuchi. They are Pashtun and are found largely in Eastern, South and Southwest Afghanistan. Here in Western Afghanistan, the camps could be semi-nomadic Turkmen, Uzbek or Aimaqs who move into yurt-like tents in the summer. In the North, the nomads tend to be nomadic Arabs, as the distrusted Pashtun Kuchis were pushed out when the Taliban fell.

Once again, we fly over Herat City. Giuseppe's team collect us at the airport and take us through town to the PRT. We have another great evening. Our hosts could not be more gracious or amicable and al fresco dining is the sunny norm here. The deal seems to be that the Spanish provide the wine and the Italians provide the food. Heaven - certainly compared to a previous experience when the French provided the beer (not wine), and the Brits provided the food.

Week Twenty
(Historic Herat, Mazar-e-Sharif, Balkh, Khulm River
Gorge, Pol-e Khumri, Salang Tunnel)

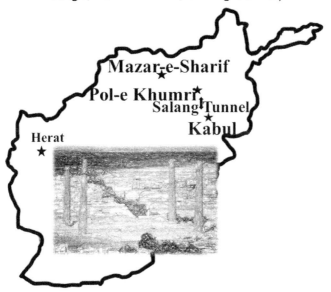

Mazar-e-Sharif

Pol-e Khumri
Salang Tunnel
Kabul

Herat

Saturday

We have a morning meeting with USAID as they
continue to play an important role in Herat.

We are short of time now before our flight but
set off to the Musalla complex with Giuseppe and his
Carabinieri team.

There are five infeasibly tall fifty-five-meter
minarets that look like factory towers and are visible all
over Herat. There are also a couple of dull mausoleums,
a ruined mosque, and a madrasa (school).

An old man greets us and purports to be a
caretaker, or a cleaner, or some such, but he might have
been just passing by. He turns out to be quite
knowledgeable.

He tells us this Timurid complex was built or started by Queen Gawhar Shad. The structures were originally ornate and magnificent and considered an architectural masterpiece of the Islamic world. There were twenty towers originally and some fell-down due to earthquakes. The destruction of most of the towers and the rest of the complex was done by the British at the end of the 19th Century. The old man said the British blew them up so they could shoot at the Russians who were expected to advance from Persia. This hugely amuses our Italian friends. Giuseppe gives the old man some Afghanis (local currency) for his trouble and off we go.

The Russians never showed-up. Luckily for the Brits there was no CNN back then to shine the spotlight of global outrage on this little-known episode.

Next stop: The Citadel. This is an immensely impressive fortress. Alexander built a fort in Herat in about 330 BCE, possibly on another site. Asiatic empires have flowed over it down the centuries. It was destroyed by Genghis Khan and his Mongol army in 1221. The Mongols spent five days just killing people – almost all the city's estimated population then of 160,000. It was rebuilt, and then destroyed again by Tamerlane and his Tartars in 1383. It was his son Shah Rukh, who rebuilt it and made it the capital of the Timurid Empire. It is now in a state of some disrepair inside with a lot of rubble everywhere. But its immense ancient walls remain intact and awe inspiring, echoing with centuries old battle cries.

Another old boy appears. He says he is a guide. He tells us of grand plans to restore the fort to its former glory. The Soviets bombed Herat heavily and indiscriminately when it was held by Mujahadeen Commander Ismail Khan, destroying huge tracts of the city, and killing thousands. Maybe the rubble is part of the mess they left behind.

Our gracious hosts drop us at the airport with much jollity, man hugs and salutes. We then fly to Kabul.

Device explodes in a vegetable kart in Kabul's Qala-e Zaman district.

Sunday

A day in the office.

Monday

Fly to Mazar-e-Sharif with Robert. His friend William Reeve joins us and proves a most wonderful and well-informed traveling companion. He has been coming here for seventeen years and lived here for six. He was a BBC correspondent covering the 2001 war from inside Taliban held Kabul. He good humouredly says John Simpson, a well-known BBC journalist, was at that time claiming to be the first Western journalist to enter the city when he did so with the Northern Alliance.

After the usual session of PRT briefings and discussions, we go into town with Colonel Russell Beattie, the PRT Commander, to see 'The Blue Mosque'. It is the Shrine of Hazrat Ali who was the fourth Caliph of the original Islamic Caliphate and is revered by Shi'ite Moslems. He was assassinated in 661 CE and is believed locally to be buried here, but most Shi'ites consider him to be buried at the Imam Ali Holy Shrine at Najaf in Iraq.

The original shrine built on the site of the Blue
Mosque in the 12th Century was destroyed by Genghis
Khan, like so much else in these parts. The present
building dates from the 15th Century. The façade, walls,
minarets, and domes are all covered in blue tiles or in
blue and white mosaics – which all gleam in the bright
sunshine. It is surrounded by a large glossy marble
plaza, fenced off at its edge with pretty railings. We do
not approach closer than these.

 A few men come and go. Some women in white
burqas can be seen in ones and twos around the
periphery. Burqas are white up here. A policeman with a
long cane-like stick swishes away a posse of boys who
shriek and run about laughing and then advance upon
him provocatively to be shooed away again.

Russell then takes us to buy carpets in a little
shop where they are piled high. I get a traditional red
Mazar-e-Sharif carpet in the Hodja Rushna style. Hodja
means someone who has studied the Quran enough to
preach or assist a Mullah and Rushna is a name. So, the

182

style is taken from the first customer or designer who was Hodja Rushna. I also get an Andkhoi runner made by Turkmen people in Northern Faryab. I get a pure silk carpet with a pink sheen from Qom in Iran, birthplace of Ayatollah Komeni, for Mariette. For Sam, whose colour is red, a small traditional deep red lamb's wool Mazar-e-Sharif Hodja Rushna. I obviously paid too much – they give me a free traditional Pakol hat and roll it up specially.

On return to the PRT, I attend their routine evening briefing session. My Gurkhas arrive safely having driven up from Kabul in our vehicles.

We then sit on a balcony in the cool of the evening and drink a cold beer. It feels like that Carlsberg they drink at the end of *'Ice Cold in Alex'*. We chat about the Australian lady tourist who was recently found somewhere north of Sheberghan looking at the stars, and the South Korean tour bus that just showed up in Kabul. It would be great to be able to come back here as a tourist. Sometimes, on an especially good day, that feels in touching distance.

At the height of the troubles in Belfast, I used to accompany my dad taking visiting business clients about Northern Ireland. They always remarked at how peaceful and wonderful it all was. My dad kept saying it was totally safe if you stayed away from the trouble spots, which was hard to square with his business premises getting bomb damaged seven times. I think he was just collateral damage. I remember on one occasion a bomb hid in a coffin went off in a hearse parked outside his offices. My mum and I went in there to help clear up and get the show back on the road.

A vehicle bomb exploded in Kandahar today killing 4 civilians.

Several rocket attacks occurred in the East killing 2 coalition soldiers.

Tuesday

The plan today is to drive to the PRT at Pol-e Khumri for evening briefings and discussions making a few pitstops along the way. Then tomorrow we will drive from Pol-e Khumri through the Salang Tunnel to Kabul.

We drive just thirty minutes west from Mazar-e-Sharif on a decent road across a landscape of dunes to Balkh. This was Bactra in the Classical period, capital of ancient Bactria. It is likely over three-thousand-years-old. For centuries it enjoyed immense prosperity as a major trading post on one of the branches of the network of Silk Routes linking India and China with Persia and the Levant.

It was a major centre of Zoroastrianism. Zoroaster (aka Zarathustra) is said to have taught, and indeed died, here. Adherents place him exactly 258 years before Alexander arrived at Balkh. But modern scholars would say he is hard to fix in time and place. Perhaps more likely sometime between 1000 and 600 BCE or even a thousand years earlier.

Zoroastrianism exalts Ahura Mazda as its all-knowing, wise but not all-powerful, supreme being. The only God worthy of worship, rather than the only God that exists. It also advocates a life path of good thoughts, good words, and good deeds centred on charitable giving. Individuals act of their own free will and are responsible for their own choices and the consequences of them. All of which sounds good to me.

It was the official religion of ancient Persia on and off for well over a thousand years until supplanted by Islam in the 7th Century. There are only a few hundred thousand followers left in the modern world. Its most famous son was probably the late and great Freddie Mercury.

Alexander the Great captured the city and campaigned around here from 329-327 BCE. He married the stunningly beautiful Bactrian princess, Roxana, to calm things down after he had Bessus, the King of Bactria, mutilated and killed. The match would also help bring her renegade father, Oxyartes, in from the cold. In my early childhood my mother gave me a Ladybird History Book of Alexander the Great. Roxana, for some reason, stuck in my mind. Now, here I am.

In the tumultuous years following Alexander's death, the Seleucid Empire was established by Seleucus, one of Alexander's generals. Bactra broke away from it in 250 BCE and became the capital of a powerful independent Greco-Bactrian kingdom. It successfully resisted a three-year siege by the Seleucids. Over the next thousand years and more, it was seized successively by Parthians, Kushans, and Sassanid Persians. In the seventh century came the Arabs and Islamification. This was followed by further evolutions in ownership by Persian dynasties and Turkic peoples from Central Asia. Sadly, despite some subsequent rebuilds and flurries of prosperity, it never quite recovered its former glories after the Mongols blew through here like a whirlwind in 1220, slaughtering the entire population.

The walls are substantially intact in many places and an impressive twenty meters or so high. They convey the sense of a walled city, not just a fortress. In and around the city is very green and fertile with many little mudbrick houses and family sized plots of land. We scramble up the walls on a sort of goat trail to take in the breath-taking views and get a sense of the enormity of all.

As we come down off the walls, we meet an old man with tidy white hair, a long beard, and an open waistcoat over the traditional loose-fitting shalwar kameez. He sends his grandson up a vine tree to fetch grapes. The old man gives them to us and thanks us for being here. He says his son has had to go to work in Iran, leaving the grandson and the son's two wives with him. I tell him *"My children's father is in Afghanistan"*.

He liked that.

We move on inside the city to the Timurid shrine of the scholar Khwaja Parsa (circa 1460). Looks sad but is still impressive with its wonderful corkscrew pillars either side of a huge arch that houses the relatively small entrance door.

The greenish blue dome is intact but there are huge patches of missing tiles all over the building. It is in desperate need of restoration. The shrine is in a beautiful park, which seems to have been looked after over the years, but it too could do with a makeover.

Beside it is the small tomb of the 9th century poetess Rabi'a Balki. It consists of a small gravestone-like plinth with an inscription. This in turn sits on a stone platform with steps down to a chamber below.

Legend has it, she was carried here by her lover Baktash, a Turkic slave soldier, after her brother slashed her wrists in a bath for shaming her family by this relationship. She wrote a love poem in her own blood as she lay dying. An honour killing mythologized with the victim transcendent:

Love
(Rabi'a Balkhi)

I am captured by your love,
Trying to escape is not possible.
Love is an ocean without boundaries,
A wise person would not want to swim in
it.
If you want love until the end
You must accept what is not accepted,
Welcome hardship with joy,
Eat poison but call it honey.

Women come and go, entering the tomb down the little steps to meditate, or pray, or just to reflect on the trials and tribulations of their own lives. We enter it briefly in a quiet moment.

We find ourselves in a small white painted stone room in which sits a plain sarcophagus draped in a green cloth. There are a couple of small-framed texts on one wall. It is attended by a little boy in traditional white garb who accepts a small donation. I ponder Rabi'a as her life ebbed away over a thousand years ago, and today the cries of those girls around Herat as they set themselves alight, and the lonely sobs of Amina in that pit as she was stoned to death.

The ruined 17th Century Madrasa of Sayid Subhan Quli Khan is at the opposite end of the little park. It is reminiscent of the ruins of a small medieval monastery or priory in Europe.

We then visit the old citadel, Bala Hissar, the fortress in the interior of the walled city. Ancient shards of pottery reportedly lie strewn around under the dust and dirt, but we don't see much of that. It gives the impression of being no more than a mound of earth, but close inspection reveals the brickwork of the once great walls.

We muse on what post conflict reconstruction might have looked like after a Mongol invasion: a centuries long project no doubt. Indeed, Persian chroniclers at the time feared Khorasan, in which Balkh then lay, would take a thousand years to recover.

We discuss what reconstruction involved after other horrendous conflicts such as the Second World War when, as now in Afghanistan, America bore the brunt of the cost with its Marshall Plan to reconstruct Europe. And the American Civil War, where a hundred years after it by the 1960s, due to unreconstructed attitudes, the descendants of the freed slaves had still not been absorbed into American society as equals.

We leave Balkh and its timeless walls sparing a thought for explorer William Moorcroft who was buried outside them in 1825. He had been to Bukhara in modern Uzbekistan searching for legendary Turcoman horses but found only Russian traders. This fueled British paranoia of Russian expansion towards their prized India and began 'The Great Game', so called, of keeping Russian influence at bay in Afghanistan. Moorcroft died at Andkhoi in Faryab province, either of poisoning or of a fever he picked up in Konduz. His men brought his body to Balkh.

Alexander Burnes found the makeshift grave on his way to Bukhara in 1832 and performed a reburial. He went on to describe the wonders of Bukhara including its busy slave market and was knighted for his exploits. He was later a political agent in Kabul during the First Anglo-Afghan War. When the Afghans turned against the Brits in November 1841 he was killed by a mob at his residence and his head displayed on a pike.

Both Moorcroft and Barnes had rather better trips to Bukhara than Stoddart and Conolly. Stoddart had already been there a few years before Conolly arrived and had endured several episodes of incarceration in the infamous 'Bug Pit' - a deep well infested with all manner of stinging, biting, repulsive crawlies. The Emir was irritated by their lack of abjectly submissive good manners toward his exalted personage and suspected they were spies. On a searing hot June day in 1842, on the vast square in front of Bukhara's majestic Ark Fortress, he had them publicly beheaded.

Their fate was uncovered in 1843 by Dr Joseph Wolff, a completely bonkers Anglican missionary of German origin, who travelled there to find them and was lucky to survive. Wolff was probably the last West European to set eyes on Bukhara until the British agent Fitzroy Maclean passed through it in 1938 on a surreptitious trip from Moscow to Kabul. He found it in a state of neglect and decline and with a red flag flying atop its charmingly named 'Tower of Death' minaret.

We drive south through a lush agricultural landscape – harvest is underway. We stop to watch children at play in filthy brown water, leaping into it off the muddy sides of a great open cistern. One in five children in Afghanistan die before their fifth birthday – mostly from dysentery and preventable diseases caused by dirty water.

A gentleman seemingly about my own age joins us. He is barefoot, in baggy shorts with a loose shirt and a makeshift turban of a small white cloth wound around his head. More children appear as if from nowhere and we are quickly swamped. He tells us with a wide smile, *"Life is good now, my children can play and go to school and I can sleep at night – thank you for being here".*

We stop very briefly at the 9th Century Masjid-i-

Hajji Piyada, which is one of the oldest examples of Islamic architecture in Afghanistan. It is a small and very dilapidated mosque. None of the original roof remains and there is deep rubble inside from the collapsed structure. A barn like roof has been erected on tall iron posts to protect what remains from the worst of the elements. Under this, a few stone columns and arches with intricate geometric and abstract patterns echo its former glory.

We quickly continue our travels which take us to Qala-i-Jangi, a large fort with low arabesque walls atop an earthen rampart. It was built by Abdul Rahman Khan, 'The Iron Emir', in 1889. He ruthlessly stabilized Afghanistan after the Second Anglo-Afghan War, putting down a series of rebellions. He also agreed the 'Durrand Line' with the British, demarking the border between Afghanistan and the frontier provinces that now lie in modern Pakistan.

The Uzbek warlord, Rashid Dostom, made the fort his headquarters when he was battling the Taliban in the mid-1990s. After the US-led intervention in 2001, Taliban fighters were held prisoner here by Northern Alliance forces loyal to him. Hundreds of them were killed in a shootout with their guards during a prison uprising. Fire also rained down from a US AC-130 gunship (basically a C130 bristling with 25 mm Gatling Guns, 40mm Bofors cannon and much else). Water was poured into the lower levels of the fort, drowning many.

There is a pall of gloom over the place. We eat our packed lunches of sandwiches and fruit, then set off for Pol-e Khumri via Aybak (Samangan).

After a long drive, in steppe-like terrain we approach the mountains and come to the enchanting Bagh-e Jahan Nama Palace. It has an attractive cluster of buildings surmounted by a white dome and surrounded by a curtain of fortress like walls. An abandoned Soviet tank litters the approach.

It too was built by Abdul Rahman Khan in the late Nineteenth Century.

We push on and happen upon the spectacular

193

Khulm River Gorge. Only yards wide. A narrow-paved road and gushing river run through it. Its sides rise vertically up and up. Breath-taking, fjord-like, and could be a set from Lord of the Rings - a giant troll might appear at any moment.

We come through the gorge to a perfect double rainbow. It straddles the now wide valley from side to side in two unbroken arcs of radiant light. The Gurkhas are very taken with this good omen and insist we stop again for photographs.

We stop briefly once more on the outskirts of Aybak and talk to some local people and a very chatty taxi driver. They are surprised to see us here. William buys cherries, which pleases the locals, and the Gurkhas wash them in their bottled water. Sadly, the day is getting away from us now, so we do not have time to explore the town or take up William's suggestion to visit the famous Buddhist caves nearby.

We arrive at Pol-e Khumri in time for a beautiful sunset. A swarm of children play football just outside the PRT.

Pol-e Khumri PRT

In the evening we hold good discussions with the leadership team. They report a great groundswell of support from locals and local leadership following the explosion incident on one of their convoys a couple of weeks ago. The incident remains a concern, despite the locals' reassurances.

During the evening meal we circulate amongst the Dutch soldiers and chat with them. They all speak better English than I do.

Later we attend a mission briefing for a patrol going into the Andarab mountains in the morning. We feel disappointed not to be going with them as we had such a great experience when we last joined a patrol from the PRT.

Wednesday

We hit the road at 0645 hours and start back on the long drive to Kabul over the Hindu Kush and through the Salang Tunnel. We pass through Pol-e Khumri bazaar, which is already bustling at that hour of the morning amid bright sunlight and long shadows.

Once out of town, the manual toil of the wheat harvest is in progress everywhere we look. We pass a drab livestock market, seemingly in the middle of nowhere. Mostly goats and donkeys. There are lots of bicycles dotted about.

Then flat plain and mile upon mile of well-ordered, water filled, green paddy fields. Men, women, and children work together, harvesting rice by hand. We wave and they wave back. A man sits in the water on a canvas director's chair making little bundles of the rice as he harvests.

We then head up into the mountains. The new

road is an excellent tarmac strip all the way with road works in progress in many places and at different stages. Lorries lay hard core, or spread tarmac, or lay grit over tarmac. Local men work with picks and shovels and big brushes. The grand plan is a mix of laying new and refurbishment of old to create a 'Ring Road' of this quality all the way round Afghanistan. I saw the far end of it in Farah. Sections have existed in various forms and states of completeness for millennia, often just as dirt tracks, and the Soviets did a lot of work on it in 1950s and 60s. This tarmac ribbon will soon reconnect Afghanistan's major cities and open-up the country as the railroads did for America, bringing goods, people, and ideas.

Soon we are at the Salang Tunnel. There is still plenty of snow about even in June and there is a great queue of lorries. On the far side of them an enterprising vendor sells piles of watermelons kept cool by melt water diverted over them by a battered strip of corrugated iron. The tunnel entrance is painted in a thick blue arc and surmounted by a portrait of Ahmad Shah Massoud in his customary pose.

Then into the tunnel itself. Just as dark as before inside but gone now are the menacing ice ruts. We are through quickly and painlessly.

The views on the south side are picture post-card stunning – distant snow, sunshine, craggy mountains, and the road winding away for miles below. We could be in Switzerland.

The long drive from the tunnel to Kabul is uneventful. As we approach the city, new homes going up look like Mediterranean villas with two or three stories set with big glass windows and attractive balconies. Then a bustling bazaar which stretches along the roadside for miles into Kabul.

Nine insurgents killed today by the Afghan National Army in clashes in Uruzgan province.

Thursday

Pow wow at the UK Embassy to discuss Counter Narcotics with senior US officials from Washington, the UK Embassy 'Drugs Team', and the visiting UK-based 'Afghan Drugs Unit'.

Evening: dinner at the Turkish Embassy. Brilliant evening. I spend most of it talking to the Chinese and Japanese ambassadors.

150 Taliban fighters killed so far this year. Cholera outbreak in Kabul – 8 dead.

Friday

Go to gym as usual. Weekly weigh-in tells me I have put on 1 lb 6 oz in my travels (0.7 KG).

Commander's birthday and birthday lunch – must dash!

Great lunch – champagne, strawberries, birthday cake and much laughter.

Week Twenty-One
(Maimana, Tarin Kot, historic Kabul)

Saturday

Waterloo day – 18th June, Duke of Wellington, and
Generalfieldmarschall von Blucher of Prussia defeat
Napoleon Bonaparte of France in what Wellington calls
'the nearest run thing you ever seen in your life'. Which,
funnily enough, is how those friends of mine who were
there describe the Falklands War.

Office day getting on with staff-work
(paperwork) we promised to deliver before leaving.

Sunday

Quiet day of routine meetings. Go with Charles
to the little carpet shop that has recently opened in the
headquarters compound. He knows his carpets. Zafar
sells me a nice one for Luke with a lot of green on it –
Luke's favourite colour and hard to come by here. It gets

wrapped in a couple of shemagh scarfs.

Office call on Peter Gilchrist in the Coalition Force Headquarters. Having run the US-led Coalition operation here for a couple of months, he now has a new US boss in Lieutenant General Eikenberry, who showed up a couple of weeks ago and wants to hear options. We have a good, wide ranging discussion.

Monday

Another office day – getting a lot done. Much preparation for tomorrow's outing to PRTs by the Executive Steering Committee (ESC).

Tuesday

We take the PRT ESC to Maimana in the ISAF area of operations and Tarin Kot in the Coalition area. Nazim comes too. About four of the Ambassadors show up in person (France, Canada, Netherlands, and Norway) the others send deputies.

Maimana is where I was stranded for eight days at the start of my tour here, so it is a bit of Alpha and Omega for me. The PRT Commander, now Lieutenant Colonel Leslie Boswell, and his Finish civilian advisor give us a brilliant briefing. They include insights into local politics, security sector improvements, security challenges, and the delivery of aid programmes in the province by numerous actors.

They describe the Shirin Tagab incident. This began with the unexpected return to the area of a minor warlord. A more pre-eminent warlord took exception and mobilized. There was a shoot-out, negotiations, another shoot-out, a shura meeting and more negotiations, then agreement. Characters like these are entering politics to be elected directly or to put forward individuals beholden to them. Good if they shout at each other rather than shoot. But it will inevitably bring more strong-arm tactics into the political arena.

We go into town to see some security sector projects, like the CID building. Then walkabout in the bazaar. Everything gets recycled here. We see tyres being made into shoes and water containers. One guy shows off his brand new little Jinhao motorbike - made in China – bright red and lots of chrome. Looks great. Says he can get us one for 500 USD. Should have bought one.

We have lunch with the Governor. We all sit at a long table and have a bowl of noodle soup (*ash*) each. There are platters of pilaf rice and smaller plates of tasty meat dishes and little pies (*sanbuseh*) and raita all down the table as well as fruit, bottles of water, cans of local Fanta and boxes of tissues. The Afghans are most amused by my travels in their country, and it helps build rapport. Some rumbles that they want to see the PRT deliver more social and welfare type projects, not just security stuff. After lunch, the governor presents us all with traditional chapan coats. I now have a minor collection of these things. The French Ambassador, Jean-Pierre Guinhut, replies in Dari on our behalf, which goes down supremely well with the Afghans.

We then fly to Tarin Kot, birthplace of Mullah Omar the leader of the Taliban. The landscape below is bleak and featureless all the way there. We land in 42 degrees Celsius in the shade, it feels extremely hot. We are taken from the airstrip to the PRT compound in a white painted South African armoured "bus". Its chassis is in a deep V to help deflect and minimize the impact of blasts from mines. The windows are narrow armoured glass slits one can barely see out of.

We have an escort of two Humvees. The compound has an earth berm all around it and then within that an eight-foot-high concrete wall with a tower in each corner. It looks like a Roman fort. We are told it cost 750,000 USD and was built with local labour.

Lieutenant Colonel Lafontaine gives us a great

briefing with his small leadership team from the US Department of State and USAID. Dyncorps provide a contracted Police Advisor, and there is an Afghan Colonel from the Ministry of Interior. Most of the seventy or so US military are Airborne Forces.

The PRT mission is to provide support to 'kinetic' combat operations. Their aim is to help create stability and security and to increase Afghan security capacities throughout Uruzgan province.

Major USAID projects include hospital repairs, roadworks, bridges, government buildings, schools, and a radio station. The military deliver numerous little projects such as wells, school repairs, agricultural equipment, fruit trees, seed, civic building repairs, police vehicles, an ambulance, and tractors.

We briefly tour the PRT, including seeing a row of little tractors awaiting issue to local farmers. We then depart as we came in a flurry of heat and dust.

Rocket attack on Farah PRT – no casualties.

Taliban seize a village in Nishim District in Kandahar - after a Shura trial they execute the Chief of Police and 7 other policemen.

Wednesday

Get on with our staff work (paperwork). Robert and I are helped greatly by staff officers from across headquarters.

Outputs include revised and much more directive orders for PRTs. A 'one size fits all' approach is not intended, but any differences between PRTs should be driven by varying situations in the provinces, not by the predilections of the countries providing PRTs.

We produce a 'Mission Essential Task List', a big deal in military bureaucracies. It specifies in detail the capabilities, resources, structures, and training required to deliver an effective PRT. A 'Best Practice' paper, which is what it says on the tin - examples of the best things each PRT is doing.

We also finalize our PRT Strategy Paper with Coalition colleagues as an offering to the PRT Executive Steering Committee.

Nazim, as Chief of Staff, sends all these up the NATO chain of command as we do not have authority to issue them locally. They will be played around with in our superior headquarters in Europe before seeing the light of day, but they seem supportive, so fingers crossed.

We also refresh and re-issue the PRT Handbook to leave an up-to-date Edition 2 in hard copies and on the NATO IT system.

In the evening, to my absolute horror, the Commander decides to open the new football pitch with a match between the Command Group and the female soldiers. Masses of troops from the headquarters turned-up to watch the floodlit match. They cram onto the rooftops and cheer wildly for the girls. Anyway, all that football in the garden with my children paid off, I have a decent game and am complimented as such – setting up our winning goal.

Thursday

On Nazim's behalf, chair a routine Video Tele-Conference with ISAF staff and their counterparts in our superior headquarters in Brunssum. Mostly just updating each other on points of detail. Nazim is tied up with the

Chief of the Turkish Army visiting today and a whole bunch of Turkish generals.

At lunch in the mass dining facility, I notice the Turkish generals are all seated together, about ten or so at a table. There is one spare seat, so I decide to join them. As I approach, I can hear them all jabbering away in Turkish. I announce myself to the visiting Army Chief, *"Merhaba Bayim, benim adim Brigadier Potts"*. Spotting that I am operating at the outer limits of my Belfast-Turkish linguistic skills, he makes an open-handed gesture of welcome and bids me to join them. In an impressive display of linguistic courtesy and urbane charm, they all switch instantly to English and include me fully in their conversation.

In the afternoon, Robert and I go out around Kabul with William Reeve, picking him up from his compound. We go to all the places we should have been to by now but have either not got to or not noticed. In truth there is much more to see than we glimpse on our whirlwind tour.

We visit the Museum of Afghanistan. It is closed. We walk round to the sad old trains at the back which are all that remains of King Amanullah's modernization efforts. He led Afghanistan against the British in the Third Anglo-Afghan War in 1919. This resulted in Britain letting go control of Afghanistan's foreign policy. It thus became fully independent in August of that year.

The British used new-fangled air power to bomb Kabul with Handley Page biplanes. They damaged bazaars and mosques and killed innocent people. Amanullah said *"It is a matter of great regret that the throwing of bombs from Zeppelins on London was denounced as a most savage act....while now we see with our own eyes that such operations is a habit which is prevalent amongst all civilized peoples of the West".* How prescient he was.

He also created schools for boys and for girls, which helped catalyze a backlash. After a rebellion he ultimately finished his days in exile in India. We also visit his dilapidated and gloomy nearby Palace, without dismounting, and move swiftly on.

Next stop, the garden and resting place of 'Babur the Conqueror'. His simple marble tomb here belies his historical importance. Babur was a descendant of Tamerlane. He lost and regained his kingdoms in the Fergana valley (in Kyrgyzstan), and Samarkand (now in Uzbekistan) three times. He removed himself to Kabul and went on to be founder of the Mogul Empire which stretched across Northern India. He wrote an extraordinary diary and memoire of his life. It captures in exquisite detail his battles, raids, hunting, partying, and his loves and fears. It records too, the lands and cities of his travels and conquests in almost Domesday Book-like detail but with artistic flair. He died at Agra, where his descendant Shah Jahan later built the Taj Mahal.

His body was brought here as he loved the place so much. The whole garden is being beautifully restored by the Agha Khan Foundation, which gives one hope.

After the brief Babur stop, we drive on. Many of the roads in the Old City are unpaved dirt tracks. The housing is squalid. Almost all the women here are in burqas. We turn off Takhta Pul Road near Hindu Street to take in the astonishing wooden mosque of Mullah Mahmood. It is an exquisite Seventeenth Century building and a hidden treasure. The US Ambassador's fund paid for its restoration and it only reopened last year. Two-stories with a seemingly flat roof. An attractive wood balustrade runs the length of the first floor. The exterior walls are a series of wooden pillars and arches infilled with wood panels and casement windows. Looks like a Swiss chalet.

Inside, the large open space is unmistakably mosque-like with rows of characteristic pillars and arches, all in wood. A few men are dotted about, praying, lying fast asleep on blankets, and in one case lying on his back having a good old stretch. They take no notice of us.

 William then takes us downtown to the 'Shah M Book Co' – a bookshop on a prominent junction near the National Directorate of Security. We had driven past it many times in these past months. The vehicles pull up right outside the door and we go in to meet William's friend, the owner, Shah Muhammad Rais. It was he and his family that Asne Seierstad lived with, recounting her experiences in 'The Book Seller of Kabul'. She named him 'Sultan Khan' in the book. William knew them both and had reviewed the book. He said Seierstad was a beautiful and engaging woman, and the book is best enjoyed as a wonderful story. I ask Shah Muhammad about her. He says curtly, *"I am taking her to court"*.

His bookshop is one of the most remarkable bookshops, indeed shops, I have ever seen. It would have been a joy to browse at leisure – another time perhaps. We do not dally despite the Gurkhas covering our backs and are in and out very quickly.

I buy Lady Sale's diary for Dinah – '*A Journal of the Disasters in Afghanistan*'. She was handed over as a hostage to Akbar Khan during the fateful retreat from Kabul and kept a detailed journal. He has numerous other Victorian era publications, all reprinted in Pakistan.

For myself, I get Nancy Dupree's incomparable '*An Historical Guide to Afghanistan*' published in 1977. Before coming here, I met lots of people who said they had been out to Afghanistan in Volkswagen Campervans and the like. They had travelled before the 1979 Russian invasion, and indeed the Iranian Revolution that same year. Tourism was sadly cauterized soon after the

Guide's publication. I also grab some nice poster-sized
photos of Buzkashi taken by Sabrina Michaud in 1974
and Whitney Azoy's definitive book on Buzkashi for my
father-in-law.

We mount-up and drive out of town past a
small herd of goats.

We turn off onto a dirt track which takes us up
'Radio Hill', so called because of the radio mast atop.
The 360-degree views are breath-taking in the now soft
evening light. It is like having a view of Kabul from a
hot air balloon. We look down on the Bala Hissar,
Kabul's ancient Citadel largely destroyed by the British
in the depredations of the Second Anglo-Afghan War.
Sadly, we do not have time to visit it, as the day is
getting away from us.

We pose for photos looking across the valley to
the long defensive wall built by the Hephthalites 'White
Huns' in the 5th Century. Looks like Hadrian's Wall. It's
about eight-meters-high and snakes away along a ridge
line into the distance.

In the evening, back at ISAF headquarters,
we have a dinner for some of the staff. I work on in the

office after dinner to about 2300.

Today the Afghan National Army retake the village where the police were executed in Kandahar. They kill 33 Taliban. This is the culmination of three days fighting in which the ANA and US-led coalition kill 102 Taliban.

Friday

Great session in the gym – I am down to 12st exactly (76.2 KG). I feel great.

Read around in my purchases.

Lady Sale is clearly one tough cookie. She would have done a much better job in 1842 of commanding the British force in Kabul than the hapless Elphinstone. She describes the weak-kneed leadership, the abominable hardship on the retreat and her own captivity. An extraordinary woman. The stuff empires are built of.

Azov sees Buzkashi as a metaphor for Afghanistan's '…*unbridled competition…chaotic, uninhibited, and uncontrollable – that lurks below the apparently cooperative surface…no one knows who will score next or fall flat.'* He also recommends *'The Horsemen'* (1971) with Omar Sharif and Jack Palance as having good Buzkashi scenes.

I notice too that Nancy Dupree refers to '*the Mongol holocaust'* – totally apt, the slaughter and destruction visited upon this region must have seemed like the end of the world at the time.

Dupree also records in Kabul, '*…. mini skirted schoolgirls…. and streams of whizzing traffic.'*

Week Twenty-Two
(Zaranj, Herat, Kabul)

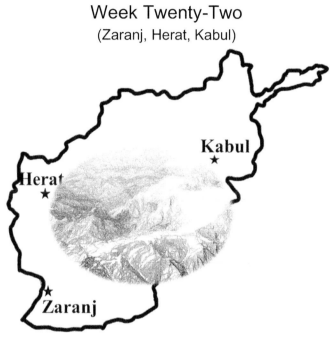

Saturday

Office-based day. Write reports and do all the stuff we have to do before leaving here.

Lots of the Brits in the headquarters and some in PRTs have asked me to write something that can be inserted in their annual appraisals. I am obviously a soft touch in this regard. I put a couple up for MBEs or OBEs (UK national recognition awards) because they deserve it. Also, because the only reason I have an MBE is that somebody bothered to write the citation.

I also write letters to the national military chains of command of some of the foreign military folks who have been particularly impressive. I write to the in-country ambassadors of some of the extraordinary civilians doing remarkable work in the PRTs, recommending their countries recognize them with national awards.

I write an effusive letter to the Gurkha's Commanding Officer letting him know they did a fantastic job and made a real impact in the headquarters.

I attend a briefing for tomorrow's recce to Zaranj on the Iranian border in the extreme Southwest of Afghanistan. The PRT Exec Committee had indicated a few potential new PRT locations and Zaranj caught the selector's eye. The Afghans are keen on it. NATO has coordinated with the Iranian authorities at the political level. The Iranians are apparently keen for a presence on the Afghan side of their border to deter and intercept illicit traffickers. The local governor and dignitaries in Zaranj are all expecting us.

A rather zealous, but amiable team have dropped down for this from our superior headquarters in Brunssum. They are led by a couple of "Tiggerish" US and UK Colonels. They and their team have been doing the detailed planning and practicing weapon drills. We have a Tactical Air Control Party with us who can call in and direct air strikes, and we have A10 'Tank Busters' and a B1 Bomber on call.

My Gurkhas are to provide close protection and Robert, the voice of professional calm in all this, promises to put a couple of extra bullets in his pocket. He talks the Gurkhas through their drills.

In the evening, the ISAF Command Group josh around getting photographed in traditional chapans draped over our uniforms (or in Suleyman's case over his smart blazer and tie). We use a room off the Commander's office which is fitted out in Turkish style with low divans and long cushions all along the walls and a couple of low coffee tables. Great craic.

We learn the sad news that two German soldiers and up to seven local civilians have been killed in Takhar province while handling ammunition and weapons handed in by warlords.

Sunday

We set off for Zaranj in a Belgian C130 at about 0530 hours. We fly over an endless vista of nothingness in the early morning light. Southwest Afghanistan is just a vast empty space.

It is also planned that while we are on the ground in Zaranj, the aircraft is to deliver a Quick Reaction Force from Herat to Farah. This is repositioning for a while due to deteriorating security generally there, rather than an urgent response to an immediate ongoing incident. Hence why we are flying to Zaranj: the overland route is just too dodgy right now.

All goes well on the flight snoozing and chatting. Until we approach Zaranj. Iranian Air Defence challenge us in bad English and threaten to shoot us down. We veer off and the aircrew talk to them. The Iranians apologize and wish us a happy landing.

On our second approach we are challenged again by a different voice, again threatening to shoot us down. We veer off once more.

There is a dust storm. We can hardly see the runway in any case. Landing will be problematic. We might even end up in Iranian airspace as the landing strip is practically in Iran.

I am asked by the pilot if I want to make a third approach. It takes me about a nanosecond to spot that we have more than thirty people on board and there is lunch to be had in Herat, so I say, "*No thanks*".

It is quickly decided we should all go to Herat so that at least the QRF redeployment part of the mission can be accomplished. This means we can have lunch with Giuseppe and the Italians in Herat; the QRF can get delivered to Farah; and we can get a message to our civic reception party in Zaranj.

Brigadier General Patang, the PRT Director General from the Ministry of Interior, is on the trip. Once we land, he calls the Provincial Governor in Zaranj, who says he is keen we try again soon. Danny Van Laethem is on the trip too. He is doubtful any of the nations would let their aircraft fly into Zaranj anytime soon. This could impact feasibility of resupply and reinforcement of any PRT setup in Zaranj, never mind another reconnaissance.

Herat is scorching hot. Our Italian friends greet their unexpected guests with their customary warmth and hospitality. We have a most wonderful early lunch of delicious pasta, pan-fried fish with crushed olives, a cold beer, and then an espresso. Possibly the best Sunday lunch in world history.

On the way back, now in a Portuguese C130, I am joined in the cockpit by Brigadier General Patang. He absolutely loves it. Again, the terrain below for the 90-minute flight is unrelentingly barren.

On landing at Kabul, we burst a tire and wobble erratically to a standstill at the end of the runway. Everyone disembarks. A small fleet of two big brand-new yellow fire engines and three white ambulances appear, all with blue lights flashing and sirens blaring. It's as if the *Thunderbirds* from International Rescue have arrived.

A group of us stand around the wheel cluster looking at the shredded tyre. Everything is fine otherwise. An Afghan interpreter says, *"Thanks goodness that didn't happen in the air"*. The Irishman in me loved that.

On return to headquarters there is much navel scratching on the Zaranj incident. It might have been a genuine low-level screw-up with the Iranian Air Defence at crew level. Could be that good will at the Iranian political level might not be transmissible through Iran's military command structure. There might even be malign vested interest groups at work in the local Iranian military. Our Afghan comrades are keen to try again in a week or two when things get straightened out with the Iranians.

Perhaps this is not an international PRT venture anyway and best left to the Afghans – their Border Police and Counter Narcotic Police and so forth.

Pack. Talk to Dinah about Jack, our wonderful English Pointer dog, who is unwell.

Monday

Attend a short memorial service for the German soldiers who were killed - Master Sergeant Christian

Schlotterhose and Sergeant First Class Andreas Heine. A nicely done service.

Suleyman Gokce, our Political Advisor, passes me and the rest of the Command Group a copy of a UN Press Release. It covers statements to the UN Security Council by Jean Arnault, Special Representative of the Secretary General to Afghanistan and Antonia Maria Costa of the UNODC. Arnault voices concern at the deteriorating security situation, especially given the upcoming elections. Suleyman also passes us all copies of his own superlative and pithy analysis of the overall situation in Afghanistan, and the role of its neighbours.

Spend afternoon wrapping presents and decanting port for my farewell dinner tonight. I brought back a fine Warre's 1975 from my cellar raided on R&R. I went to Sandhurst in 1975 so this farewell dinner will be almost 30 years to the day and good use of the port.

Farewell pizza lunch in the headquarters garden with George White and a colleague of his from the US Embassy. George and I had enjoyed a great cooperation. It seems nuts for me to be going after such a relatively short time. There is a job to do providing a bit of leadership to all these PRTs and helping to manage interfaces in Kabul with entities the PRTs deal with in the provinces. It would be best done by someone who can be here for a couple of years or more to build relationships and provide some continuity. If they had sufficient notice of being sent here, they might even learn the lingo rather than just pick-up fragments as they go along.

Farewell dinner with the Command Group. Nice speech by the Commander. He gives me heaps of wonderful Turkish gifts and pins a medal on me. I hand out signed copies of my book 'Command and Combat in the Information Age' and a CD that I made of slides they can use if they wish to give talks on Afghanistan in their home countries. I give the Commander a Gurkha Kukri Knife engraved on the blade 'to LTG Ethem Erdagi from Potts Pasha' he loved that, and so did the team. The port went down a treat and cigars were handed round. Great evening.

I call home and learn that Jack has been put to sleep – kidney failure.

Dinah has handled the whole thing wonderfully.

Luke tells me, "Jack's kidneys don't work anymore so he has been put to sleep and he is dead now and he won't be coming home".

Mariette says, "I want Jack back, I don't want no dog" and "It's all mummy's fault".

Sam says, "Hi dad, I hope nobody else gets sick before you come home".

And there you have it – a master class in differing perspectives and a metaphor for these past months here.

Tuesday

Gym – still 12 stones (76.2 KG).

Hot day in the office.

In my final days here, I share a few thoughts on all this from my parochial perspective.

This operation might be edging towards a successful strategic outcome if all this development activity can take hold and we deliver a functioning security sector. This would be of historic significance – as indeed would failure.

Success hinges on remaining engaged, matching resources to the immense scale of the task, and staying focused on an exit strategy. ISAF's exit is best predicated on delivering effective indigenous security structures, including police who are the first line of defence. For PRTs to exit, we need to understand what not being needed looks like and work towards that.

Threats to success are narcotics; corruption; lack of indigenous capacity; donor fatigue because there is so much left to do; and the situation in Pakistan, a safe haven for the Taliban, which threatens to unstitch our best efforts here.

NATO expansion around Afghanistan also threatens success, given its fragmented effort and military-centric approach. It often seems is as if its counterclockwise expansion around Afghanistan and generating the force contributions from nations to fulfill that (who goes where and who commands what) is its consuming strategic objective, rather than how to reach some sort of end game.

In the bigger picture, there is a lot of chat amongst the politicos on the diplomatic circuit of a

'Versailles Syndrome' at the Presidential Palace. Bad news is not received, horizons close into the palace walls and adverse developments in the countryside are not recognized. If true, this does not bode well.

A heroin industry, on the scale of Columbian cocaine, has metastasized throughout the country and the prospect of Afghanistan becoming a 'narco-state' is very real. Helmand and Nangahar are by far the worst offenders for poppy cultivation with Kandahar, Badakhshan, Farah and Uruzgan in the next tier. The Russians said a couple of weeks ago that heroin production in Afghanistan threatens the whole world.

'Alternative Livelihoods' for poor farmers enmeshed in poppy continues to lag and is now a litmus test issue for overall success or failure here. The value to the farmer of an alternative crop need only exceed the price for poppy paid to him by the warlord, 'the farm gate price'. This is much lower than the value of the processed heroin product, let alone the 'street price' in Europe. There is also a mesh of debt and obligation between the farmers and the warlords that will be tricky to untangle.

Unfortunately, narcotics, corruption, and lack of indigenous capacity are all enmeshed and stymie progress in the provinces.

'Disarming Illegal Armed Groups' grinds on but to questionable effect with weapons collection merely inviting an endless round of gestures by often dangerous and devious characters. The people want this to happen, but it is a 'big ask' given an estimated 1800 or so armed groups across the country.

An Afghan Government led reconciliation process 'Program-e Tahkem-e Solh' is now underway to

reintegrate Taliban and other Islamist fighters who
renounce violence. About a hundred and fifty have
'come in' as it were, so far. Early days but already
looking like a candle in the wind.

The security situation is deteriorating week on
week with incidents increasing in both number and
seriousness – some 300 in the past 3 months, which is a
lot, but Iraq is currently running at 400 incidents a week.
The negative security situation here can be expected to
intensify as Afghanistan's September elections loom. It
is hard to judge right now whether this is a summer
fighting season and election year phenomenon or a
longer-term adverse trend.

The Afghan National Army, with Embedded
Training Team support, is showing it can beat the
Taliban in tactical engagements, which is good news and
something to really build on. Indeed, it is often said how
tough the Afghans are, as though that is a reason not to
be here or not to fight them. But the ANA are Afghans
too and so are the long-suffering Afghan people and we
are on their side.

Pack, talk to Dinah, attend BBQ in garden.
Pack.

US CH47 Chinook shot down in Kunar
province, Eastern Afghanistan, all sixteen people on
board missing, feared dead.

Wednesday
0700 – Kabul International Airport – we all
salute in respectful observance of coffins being loaded
onto a flight for Germany. They are not just lost German
soldiers today, but International soldiers:

222

'...did they beat the drum slowly, did they play the fifes lowly, did they sound the death march...and did the band play the last post and chorus?'

SACEUR arrives – routine visit, purely coincidental with everything that is going on.

Session with David Copeland and Andrew Kennet, peers of mine from the UK Permanent Joint Headquarters.

Evening: farewell dinner with James Denny and the Brits at Camp Souter. David and Andrew being in town helps with the timing. We eat like kings: Carpaccio of Beef Salad, Pan Fried 'Lobster' Tail, Coffee Pavlova, and a glass of 'The House Red'. The crustaceans are a collateral benefit of having Nordics in our supply chain.

Thursday

Final packing.

Check-in baggage at Kabul airport. My backpack and large hold-all get palletized. I am now to travel and get by for tonight on 'hand baggage' only, which gives the trip a budget airline feel.

Close office - farewells etc.

Friday

Walk to the headquarters building in the bright morning sunshine to meet with my vehicles and team. Robert is to return with me. The rest of the team have not been here long and are to be absorbed back into the Camp Souter structure and the Gurkha battalion.

I arrive to find my team already there plus the Commander who has come out to say a final farewell.

We are soon joined by the rest of the Command Group. We chat and shake hands for one final time. It feels very odd to be going.

The moment arrives when we must depart. We drive out of the camp past the rag-tag Friday market and through the camp gates into the teeming throng of humanity that is Kabul, and on to the airport.

Then we fly home.

In Central Afghanistan, the Afghan National Army attack a Taliban hideout killing eighteen. Two ANA soldiers lose their lives.

In Kunar province, Eastern Afghanistan, a US airstrike kills forty-eight civilians including twenty-five from an extended family attending a wedding reception.

Afterword

On Friday 7th July 2005, exactly one week after I left Afghanistan, the so called 7/7 bombings occurred in London. Four young British jihadists blew themselves to pieces, killing 52 others and injuring 700 in the process. Their online testimonies said they had been inspired by the leaders of Al Qaeda (now holed-up in Pakistan) and by 'Al Qaeda in Iraq'.

I had plenty of scope in Afghanistan compared to most military who are confined to a headquarters or a sand box. But by the end of my short time there I felt I had hardly scratched its surface and had almost whizzed around it on a magic carpet.

My overall impression was of a most wonderful country with harsh geography of immense scale and great depths of history. Dangerous too with a constant atmosphere of menace. It is populated by tough people, as hard as nails with lived-in faces but hallmarks of kindness and humility.

There were many visible improvements from the enormous reconstruction and development efforts: roads, airports, power supply, telecommunications, hospitals, schools, administrative buildings, better access to clean water, mine clearance, reintegration of refugees, and elections with high levels of female participation. Impressive achievements. This gave hope to the people, but the scale of the need seemed bottomless.

In the countryside, agriculture flourished in many areas and there were bustling bazaars. Myriad

towns and villages of simple mudbrick dwellings had
hardly changed in millennia. Some were peppered with
satellite dishes and mobile phone use was commonplace.
It was as if the Twenty-First Century was melding with
the Eleventh, or even the First. But the major cities
could have been busy hubs of developing economies
almost anywhere.

The job I went to after Afghanistan required
periodic brief trips there. I had fleeting 'fly on the wall'
glimpses of both the Italian and British-led ISAFs in
Kabul. The PRTs that had been my remit were now
taken under the wings of the ISAF Deputy Commanders.
After the Brits, the rotation of ISAF leadership between
NATO nations stopped. All the Commanders thereafter
were Americans and there was an influx of US staff into
the headquarters. It is as if NATO didn't quite take over
and instead the US effort absorbed ISAF.

I also saw something of the Brits in Helmand
and Kandahar. The fighting was fierce. There was no
strolling around bazaars. The place was a war zone. At
the peak of the fighting, there were 8,000 Afghan
National Army and 30,000 ISAF troops in Helmand, of
which 20,000 were US Marines.

On one trip we got flown out of Kandahar via
Oman on a little British HS125 jet, normally reserved
for politicians and royalty. Once airborne in our dusty
combat gear, an RAF chap in starched uniform served us
a Gin & Tonic. Surreal, straight out of '*Catch-22*'.

Ultimately there were twenty-seven PRTs across
Afghanistan's thirty-four provinces. A few became

civilian-led including in Helmand and Konduz. Many had various evolutions in national ownership, some of which was trailed in the narrative.

The Swedes took over in Mazar-e-Sharif and the Norwegians in Maimana.

The Danes didn't take over in Faisabad. Instead, they went South to Lashkar Gah with the Brits and Estonians.

The Lithuanians went into Chagcharan and were joined by Danes, Icelanders, Georgians, Ukranians and Americans.

The Hungarians took on Pol-e Khumri, freeing the Dutch to take over Tarin Kot from the US. It later reverted to the US, this time along with the Australians.

South Korea took on the US PRT at Bagram, covering Parwan Province.

Turkey provided the twenty-seventh PRT, which went into Maidan Shar in Wardak Province.

Three potential new PRT locations were mentioned in the narrative. The US went into the fiercely independent Panjshir. None was provided to Dai Kundi or Zaranj, which from an ISAF perspective remained on the periphery of the known world.

PRTs continued to be divergent. The many different 'lead nations' had their own ideas as to what they were doing in Afghanistan and hugely different risk appetites. Different local situations persisted from province to province too, providing a rationale, and in some cases a pretext, for differing approaches.

PRTs were controversial, but they delivered a long list of benefits to Afghans. Provincial Governors were often wedded to them and they were popular with local people. Those who served in them have a lot to be proud of.

President Karzai announced in 2011 that PRTs had become parallel structures inhibiting the development of Afghan capacity and were to close by 2014. Next year, in 2012, NATO announced that ISAF would fold by the end 2014 anyway. PRTs duly closed and became 'dust in the rear-view mirror'.

The multi-billion-dollar development and security reform effort carried on. The US Congress alone appropriated 125 Billion USD in aid for Afghanistan to 2018. As well as big ticket items and national scale programmes costing hundreds of millions of dollars, there were also myriad smaller scale cultural and humanitarian activities. The narrative mentioned some of the wonderful restoration work by the Agha Khan Foundation and UNESCO. MSF returned to Afghanistan in 2009 and established maternity units in Khost in Eastern Afghanistan and in a hospital in Kabul. The Red Cross's Alberto Cairo and his team had by 2019 assisted an incredible 100,000 Afghan amputees.

But delivering even basic health care, education, roads, and especially universal adult suffrage, brought great changes that would challenge any traditional society. Anything that improved the lot of women was an especial challenge in Afghanistan and something of a litmus test of progress.

The position of women remains precarious particularly when trying to access justice. There is a national criminal justice system and locally dispensed justice through traditional Shuras, which are an especial risk for women. As recently as 2013, to placate traditionalists, Karzai's government toyed with introducing stoning into the Afghan penal code but backed off rapidly in the face of international reactions. It was then banned.

Acts of misogynistic violence continue. In 2019 the Afghan Independent Human Rights Commission recorded 96 honour killings. Some individual incidents are shocking. In October 2020, a young woman (Khatera aged 33) was stabbed in the eyes and blinded in Ghazni province for taking a job in the police without her father's consent. In March 2021, three women working on a polio immunization programme were shot dead.

There are now many women in public life and numerous strong female role models. There are female government ministers, provincial governors, members of parliament, senior police and army officers, and even an Air Force fast jet pilot. As education works through, women are entering professions.

Culture, media, and sport have flourished too, providing avenues of advancement for many women and an air of normalcy for all. Afghan cinema provides a window into a country otherwise inaccessible to most. The 2011 movie *Buzkashi Boys* tells a story of unfulfilled dreams and includes beautifully shot scenes of Buzkashi in the quite rustic form I witnessed in 2005.

March 2021 saw the second National Buzkashi League in Kabul with teams from sixteen provinces. It was covered live on RTA (national Radio Television Afghanistan) by a team that included a female commentator. A female solo artist belted out songs in the intervals. There were fewer 'chapandaz' (riders) in each team than I had witnessed, an umpire now rode about armed with a whistle and a yellow card for sending off offending players, and there were boundary lines and a cage fence to protect the crowd. It was a magnificent spectacle, nonetheless. The final between Konduz and Kandahar ended in a controversial 3:3 draw. 'Marshal' Rashid Dostom presided.

Cricket is now one of Afghanistan's most popular sports with over three hundred clubs across the country. The national team achieved 'One Day International' status in 2009. In January 2021 they beat Ireland in Dubai.

But lurking below this engaging veneer of normalcy are some grim realities. Heroin remains a multi-billion-dollar industry and an all-pervading corrupting influence at every level of Afghan society. The Taliban switched from banning poppy to deriving an estimated 60% of their income from it, thus entwining narcotics and terrorism.

The UNODC 2020 report says 2019 was a bumper poppy harvest and that both the Eradication and Alternative Livelihoods programmes have now virtually ceased. It also reported that if Helmand were a country, it would be the world's largest heroin producer.

General Doud, whom we met in the narrative leading the Counter Narcotics charge, went on to be Chief of Police in Northern Afghanistan. He was murdered by the Taliban and the Al Qaeda affiliated Islamic Movement of Uzbekistan on 28 May 2011.

DIAG, the Disarming of Illegal Armed Groups, has had mixed results. Several hundred groups have been disarmed but hundreds more remain. An Afghan Ministry of Interior report in 2019 said some 50,000 weapons and millions of bullets have been handed in since 2008. There have also been some high profile and unlikely successes along the way in tough provinces like Panjshir and Nangahar. Afghanistan's only female warlord was voluntarily disarmed in Baghlan. A policy was introduced of forming local militias to help fight the Taliban. This seemed to run counter to the spirit of DIAG by enabling members of illegal armed groups to re-invent themselves and remain armed.

The Afghan National Police grew to a 116,000 strong force. EUPOL took over from the Germans in 2007 and drove reform in the Ministry of Interior. Successes included a Police Staff College and a confidential hotline for reporting crime. The EUPOL mission closed in 2016 having handed over its initiatives to the Afghans.

EUPOL also helped produce the Afghan police drama series *Commissar Amanullah* with its strong anti-corruption message. Its director and Amanullah's female boss in the series, Saba Sahar, a women's rights activist, and real-life police Colonel, was ambushed and shot in the stomach four times in August 2020; she fought back and survived.

The US effort to deliver a police force on the ground and at scale passed from the US Department of State to Defense. Some argue this contributed to the police being militarized into a para-military force, detracting from the development of effective community policing. Equally, militarization was necessary for survival as the police suffered greatly from attacks by the Taliban. Unfortunately, a reputation for corruption and complicity in the heroin industry undermined the ANP's legitimacy and inhibited its ability to be an effective partner.

The Afghan National Army grew from around 20,000 in 2005 to about 180,000 by 2014. It has conducted numerous successful military operations and assisted communities in disaster relief. ISAF provided it with US Embedded Training Teams and NATO Operational Mentor and Liaison Teams to help with on-the-job training, planning and combat support. There are many brave and dedicated men and women in it, but it has been riddled with corruption. Manpower was inflated to collect 'ghost' salaries, and equipment and supplies, especially fuel, sold on to third parties. Worst of all, its soldiers sometimes killed their US and NATO comrades. The Afghans assess it would need to be 260,000 strong if foreign forces withdrew, but it will struggle to get there due to high rates of desertion and low uptake of annual re-enrollment.

Corruption stunted progress in every aspect of the Security Reform and development effort and paradoxically was fueled by billions of dollars in poorly accounted for aid. Reams of reports document the diversion of aid money to warlords, corrupt officials, politicians, and Western contractors.

Transparency International's 2005 Corruption Perception Index (CPI) rated Afghanistan at 118 out of 159 countries listed, not too bad. But since then, it consistently rated as one of the most corrupt countries in the world. The 2020 CPI put it 165th of 180 countries - equal with Guinea Bissau and immediately above Haiti and the Democratic Republic of the Congo. Numerous initiatives through Presidential proclamations, ministerial actions, successive commissions, and specialist anti-corruption police units have not stemmed it. Corruption helped ensure Afghanistan sucked in an immensely complex international effort and its considerable bags of gold, without always delivering commensurate outcomes.

By the time I went to Afghanistan, Iraq was already a 'Black Hole' for resources and attention. We went into Afghanistan in October 2001. We attacked Iraq very soon after in March 2003. The subsequent violent chaos in Iraq catalyzed upheaval across the Middle East, North Africa and beyond. It absorbed military resources, finances, and political attention span at a time when Afghanistan needed enormous resources and a sustained focus. This was especially so in the critical years 2005-8 when the Iraq war peaked, and the Taliban 'insurgency' intensified.

The Iraq war also caused Al Qaeda in Iraq (AQI) to come into being as a hideously effective terrorist force. It later expanded into Syria and morphed into Islamic State. It split with Al Qaeda and became a globalized brand superseding Al Qaeda as the germinator of jihadists world-wide. IS offshoots have been active in Afghanistan committing many heinous attacks. This included in May 2020 a deliberate gun attack on mothers and babies in the MSF maternity wing of a Kabul hospital killing 24. The Taliban remain close to Al Qaeda, so IS are its jihadi rivals, but IS has brought great pain to the Afghan people and acted as a violent accelerant.

We were in over our heads already in Afghanistan, as it turned out, and then became even more so in Iraq. The Iraq War stymied prospects for both a successful outcome in Afghanistan and for screwing the lid back onto the jihadist jar.

The high-water mark of military and political engagement in Afghanistan was President Obama's 2009-12 troop surge. This took US troop numbers to 102,000 and the rest of NATO to 38,000 at its 2011 peak. That year, they and the Afghan people faced some 3,346 terrorist attacks.

The surge was accompanied by a strong personal message from Obama to Karzai on tackling corruption and a US initiated political process to reconcile the Afghan Government and the Taliban. Diplomatic efforts to promote regional stability and aid efforts were ramped up too. There was a vigorous effort to target Taliban and Al Qaeda leadership in Pakistan, culminating in the killing of Osama Bin Laden in May 2011.

Thousands of Taliban were killed in large-scale battles, but they kept coming back. ISAF killed a lot of civilians too, boosting Taliban recruiting. Raids on peoples' homes caused outrage as soldiers sometimes entered women's bedchambers or netted the innocent.

After the surge, troop numbers reduced rapidly. NATO ceased combat operations on 28 December 2014 and folded ISAF. A revised mission would provide limited military assistance to the Afghans.

A surge can be waited out by an opponent, operating on longer time scales. I had not been following Afghanistan closely at the time, but I remember feeling surprised by news of a surge and thinking that a longer-term sustainable level of commitment made more sense.

Most Army officers of my vintage remained connected to events in Afghanistan through links to their old regiments. The brave young men and women in mine suffered their share of deaths and horrific life changing injuries.

It is sobering to consider the human cost of all this through the lens of the death toll to end 2020. Some 43,000 Afghan civilians and 64,000 local military and police were killed. Over 3,500 international military lost their lives, mostly between 2006 and 2014.

The conflict is demonstrably Afghan on Afghan. They have borne the brunt of it with over 100,000 deaths. Horrific though that number is, it is less than a tenth of Afghan deaths during the war with the Soviets and is likely less than the number who died fighting each other after the Soviets left. Afghanistan has become the graveyard of Afghans rather than the graveyard of empires.

The Human Rights Watch 2020 report catalogues the deaths caused by the 1,750 terrorist attacks that took place in 2019, the highest number since the 2011 peak. But disturbingly it also asserts that in the same period more Afghan civilians were killed by air strikes.

The US lost some 2,300 troops killed; the deepest pool of blood spilt by any foreign force. They lost 4,424 in Iraq where force levels were much higher. In historic terms, both are low losses compared to what now seems an incredible 36,000 US military deaths in Korea (1950-53) and 50,000 in Vietnam (1955-73).

For the UK, 454 dead. Comparatively, UK lost 519 in Malaya (1948-60) a slow burn, 255 in the Falklands, 179 in Iraq, and 722 military in Northern Ireland, excluding local forces. In terms of the intensity of the tactical fighting, more akin to Korea perhaps where UK lost 1100.

Canada lost 157, having taken on Kandahar, one of the most significant and hotly contested provinces.

They had not experienced combat since Korea, where they lost 516.

France lost 88 dead in some ferocious fighting. Ten paratroopers were killed in the Surobi ambush near Kabul. This shook France's military confidence and caused a rethink of approach and tactics. Historically, in Korea they lost 262, but a breath-taking 20,000 French troops were killed in Indochina (their Vietnam war) (1946-54) and at least 17,000 in Algeria (1954-62).

The Nordics lost 60 of which Denmark accounted for 43 – the highest per capita loss of any NATO country. Danish public support for involvement remained high throughout.

For the Germans, deploying forces outside their country, firstly in the Balkans and then Afghanistan, created significant political and constitutional issues for them. They lost 54 military and 3 police. Public dismay led to the introduction of a 'Cross of Honour' to recognize the bravest of the brave.

Turkey lost 15, mostly in accidents. A mercifully low number for them having provided security in Kabul, ISAF leadership twice, and a PRT. They lost 898 in Korea and have suffered over 5,000 military killed fighting Kurdish separatists since 1978.

Italy lost 53, Australia 42, Spain 35, the Netherlands 25 – the list goes on, as ultimately some fifty countries took part in ISAF.

Add to the death toll the immense cost in horrendous life changing injuries, mental trauma, the collateral of family breakdown and maladjustment of returning soldiers. For some countries in ISAF, not usually participants in foreign interventions, their losses and trauma were a disproportionate shock.

Despite losing an estimated 70,000 dead, the Taliban are unlikely to go away anytime soon. Their zealotry is incomprehensible to the rational mind. They seem to meld religious fanaticism, akin to early Christian martyrs or the medieval Shi'ite Assassins, with the maniacal cruelty of the Nazis or the Khmer Rouge.

The Taliban are now terrorizing people in much of the country. The Long War Journal (LWJ) tracks Taliban control at district level. It assesses that broadly 20% of districts are under Taliban control, including Southern Helmand; 30% are under the government; and 50% are 'contested', including the rest of Helmand. The government controls the capital and provincial centres, although some have at times been briefly seized by the Taliban, including Farah and Konduz.

Militarily, the LWJ reports the situation is something of a stalemate. The Taliban can commit acts of terrorism in the major cities, including Kabul, but are unlikely to be able to seize and hold them anytime soon. Nor in the near-term is the government likely to retake those areas controlled by the Taliban.

As part of President Trump's deal to withdraw US forces by May 2021, the Taliban gave some commitments including not to allow Afghanistan to yet again be a spawn-centre for international terrorism. Nevertheless, they retain close links with Al Qaeda who are active in parts of Afghanistan, including in Helmand, something the Taliban deny.

Everywhere the Taliban now take control, people who helped internationals, or worked for the

Afghan state, or advanced democracy, those who taught girls in school and girls who went to school, are all at risk of terrible abuse. The degree of retribution and reimposed restrictions seems to vary from district to district at the discretion of local Taliban commanders, but let us not imagine that any of them have a 'live and let live' disposition.

As the Trump deal's May deadline for troop withdrawal approached, 10,000 troops from 36 countries remained in Afghanistan, including 2,500 US and 1,300 Germans – the second largest contribution. The Afghan government said it has never needed foreign military support more. NATO said May is too soon for a 'responsible withdrawal' and that the Taliban must live up to their commitments.

President Biden then announced on 14 April that the US would withdraw its troops without preconditions by September 11th - twenty years after 9/11. NATO said it will withdraw in tandem. The stated logic is that conditions if unfulfilled snare the US there indefinitely and that a military presence no longer adds to the resolution of the conflict. A presence will apparently be retained 'in the region' to strike at any emerging direct threat to the US and its allies – absent a ground force this presumably means someone will get bombed.

The US previously committed to its substantial share of bank rolling Afghanistan's Security Forces to at least end 2024. They and other donors have also pledged 12Bn USD in aid until then. Secretary of State Blinken reaffirmed the US position on aid in Kabul on 15 April.

Nevertheless, there is a real spectre of losing hard-won gains: of state collapse, Taliban rule, and the re-establishment of international jihadist bases in the country – which CIA Director Burns said on 14 April was a real risk. There are echoes too of the West losing interest in Afghanistan after the Soviets left.

For their part, the Taliban have just declined to attend a US sponsored dialogue in Istanbul while foreign forces are based in their country. So far this month they have killed 18 civilians and 72 pro-government forces. In the worst incident near Lashkar Gah in Helmand they killed 10 soldiers and took 12 others prisoner.

Whether foreign forces finally withdraw or not on any given date, and how the Taliban choose to react is largely symptomatic. Resolving the conflict requires either compromise between the Afghan belligerents, or for one or another side to prevail.

Mullahs and Ulema across Afghanistan have said reaching agreement is an Islamic duty. Numerous interlocutors - Russia, Iran, Turkey, Qatar, and others - have stepped up efforts to help the Afghans negotiate. We shall see whether the Taliban can compromise sufficiently on the religious and social objectives of their Jihad (Holy War); and how, if at all, they can then be accommodated in an Afghan state. Compromising on matters of faith and fundamentalist religious dogma will be much trickier than compromising politically.

The Taliban are just as likely to try to win once the US and their allies have gone or as they ease out of the door. Other jihadist groups, not part of any dialogue, will continue to commit atrocities and might attract discontented Taliban. The interests of ruthless narco-warlords are served by continuing instability and for many fighters, violence is now an ingrained way of life. Bloody ethnic and tribal fault lines and an accumulation of scores to settle add to the volatile mix. The circling regional players in this tough neighbourhood can choose to be constructive or make mischief. Not a great outlook.

I did not leave Afghanistan feeling that failure was inevitable, indeed I was quite optimistic. In truth that was more a function of my 'glass half full' personality than any objective assessment. We were not there to create a Switzerland, just a country strong enough to stop Al Qaeda and the Taliban from coming back. A 'big ask' as it turned out amid many competing international priorities and at times the lack of an effective partner in the Afghan government.

This long, brutal, and at times forgotten Afghan war has soaked up treasures that have become harder to afford and cost many lives. The end seems in sight for foreign forces, but it is certainly not yet over for the Afghan people. Their country has now been mired in a near continuous state of warfare for over forty years. History will judge whether it needed to be that way.

Terrible Recent History 101

The Soviets had a lot of influence in Afghanistan in the 1960s and 70s. They undertook major infrastructure projects, such as the 'Ring Road' and the Salang Tunnel, and trained and equipped the Afghan Armed Forces. The Soviet Union was aligned with India, so Pakistan didn't like this much.

Afghan Communists then took over the country in a 1978 coup. Their anti-opposition pogrom and brutal enforcement of secular Marxist ways provoked a violent backlash. Factional infighting within the Communist regime added to the instability and chaos. The Soviets invaded in 1979 to set things straight. This became a complete mess.

A patchwork of Afghan 'Mujahadeen' guerilla fighters were supported by the US, UK, Saudi Arabia, Iran, Pakistan, and many others. A proxy war developed between the Soviets and the US (see *Charlie Wilson's War*). The US and Saudis pumped-in hundreds of millions of dollars in weaponry annually. This poured petrol on the fire and both intensified and prolonged the conflict. Individuals came to fight from across the Moslem world and included Osama Bin Laden.

The Soviets tried bombing the people in the countryside into submission. Both sides committed atrocities. The fighting resulted in 1.5 million Afghan deaths and over three million refugees, mostly to Iran and Pakistan, plus a further two million displaced persons within Afghanistan. Ultimately, the Soviets withdrew in 1989 having lost at least 15,000 dead (maybe 75,000), possibly half a million sick and injured, and billions of dollars in resources. The stress of the war contributed to the collapse of the Soviet Union, but there were a great many other more determinant factors.

Those who saw the Soviet Union as an existential threat to the West will likely argue that showering money and weapons on the Mujahadeen made sense at the time. The Soviet writer Alexander Prokhanov wrote in 1989 that *"the threat of militant fundamentalism remains a reality....it is quite strange that those who provide most of the arms to this particular camp do not understand that such a regime is equally hostile to socialism and Western structures, and even to Muslim traditionalism."* How prescient he was.

A Soviet-backed government under Najibullah wobbled on until 1992. The Mujahadeen-backed parties took over at this point in a power sharing arrangement. Najibullah took refuge in a UN compound in Kabul.

Gulbuddin Hekmatyar's Hesb-e Islami Mujahadeen group did not join the government. Equipped by Pakistan, they rained rocket and artillery fire down on Kabul destroying much of the city. Saudi Arabia and Iran supported rival factions, who soon started fighting each other. Much of the country, especially the South, was controlled by local warlords. Chaos reigned.

The warlords had been Mujahadeen commanders, and they supplanted traditional sources of authority in rural communities. After the Soviet departure, these commanders became oppressive local tyrants; many were just gangsters.

Into this mix, almost from nowhere, stepped the Taliban who promised to rid the country of warlords.

They had developed their distinct brand of Islamic fundamentalism in Madrasas (Islamic schools) of the Deobandi sect in Pakistan. They sought to return Afghanistan to Islam's purist Seventh Century form and believed social justice and order would be realized by doing so.

They were influenced by Al Qaeda, who were also ensconced in Pakistan, and who enmesh their own kind of Saudi derived Wahhabi fundamentalism with the violent ideology of Political Islam's most extreme radicals, like the Egyptian Sayyid Qutb. They sought to renew the entire Islamic world by returning it to its fundamentals through violent jihad.

The Taliban were much less intellectualized and much more parochial. They entwined Afghan traditionalism, specifically the Pashtun tribal social code of Pashtunwali, and Pashtun ethno-nationalism. But they are not all Pashtuns, nor are they Pashtun separatists. Their credo is shaped too by the emphatic rejection of colonialism, a visceral reaction to the horrors inflicted by the Soviets, and extreme disappointment at the failure of the Mujahadeen to deliver a stable and just Islamic society in Afghanistan.

Social order was needed urgently. The Taliban intended to impose it through strict application of Islamic Sharia Law, presided over by their priestly caste of fundamentalist mullahs.

The Taliban had also become the prime client of Pakistan's Inter-Services Intelligence (ISI) agency which was itself riddled with fundamentalists. ISI wanted sympathetic Pashtun fighters in charge in Kabul and now thought the Taliban were the best candidates rather than Hekmatyar and others they had backed hitherto. ISI enabled Taliban training in Pakistan and their recruitment activities in the teeming Afghan refugee camps there.

The Taliban seized Kandahar in 1994 and then took other areas in the South. They were initially welcome in many Afghan communities as they offered to put an end to warlords and provide stability - something people genuinely craved.

After defeats around Kabul by Mujahadeen forces under Ahmed Shah Massoud, and in the approaches to Herat in the West by Ismael Khan, they lost momentum until Pakistan stepped-up support. The Taliban then seized Herat and later Kabul. In September 1996 they announced their 'Islamic Emirate of Afghanistan'.

They dragged former President Najibullah from the UN compound in Kabul, castrated him and his brother and hung them from some traffic lights.

These events catalyzed the formation of the 'Northern Alliance' of all anti-Taliban forces of all ethnicities and increased their foreign support. Iran supported Ismael Khan, Russia and Uzbekistan supported Rashid Dostom, and Russia and Iran supported Ahmed Shah Massoud.

The Afghan Armed Forces had completely fragmented so these premier league warlords commanded large elements of them and had tanks, artillery, helicopters, and even some MiG fighter-bombers. The Taliban were supported by Bin Laden's Arab and Central Asian fighters; by Saudi Arabia with money and hundreds of new pick-up trucks; and by Pakistan with training, thousands of individual Pakistani fighters, Army Commandos deployed into Afghanistan, weaponry, and bombing raids. Carnage ensued.

The Taliban combined lightening advances in columns of pick-up trucks with bribery of rivalrous factions to shift their allegiances, intimidation, and massacres. They took control of the country less for the far Northeast corner where Massoud held out. The Shi'ite Hazaras had an especially tough time and were subjected to slaughter and starvation.

Areas controlled by the Taliban lived under heinous tyranny, which was especially directed at women. The gap between the Taliban's laudable vision of salvation from the predations of warlords and the reality of their misrule could not have been greater. The education, health and public administration systems collapsed along with other vestiges of organized society and economy.

Afghanistan also became a safe haven for Al Qaeda. From there they plotted the 1998 bombings of the US Embassies in Nairobi and Dar es Salaam, the 9/11 attacks on the US, and much else. A hotch-potch of other violent Jihadist groups gravitated around the Taliban in Afghanistan and in the camps in Pakistan.

The country was a dystopian wasteland by the time the 9/11 attacks tipped the world into the US-led intervention and the subsequent stabilization and development efforts.

NATO Command Structure 101

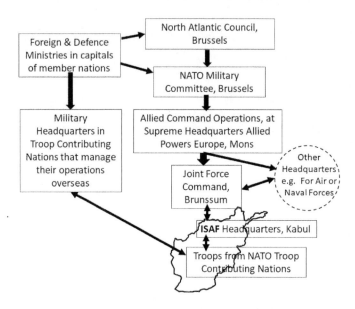

NATO is an alliance of nations. The nations collectively decide what the alliance will do. The bureaucratic structure basically brokers, convenes, corrals, implements, and manages assigned forces and operations.

The North Atlantic Council (NAC) is NATO's supreme decision making and governing body. Ambassador-level 'Permanent Representatives' at NATO Headquarters in Brussels, chaired by Secretary General. Can meet at higher level: Ministers for Defence or Foreign Affairs or Prime Ministers/Presidents of member nations. Foreign and Defence Ministries maintain close contact with their representatives.

The NATO Military Committee (NMC) sits below the NAC and provides it with military advice.

General Officers, usually Three-Star, assigned to NATO
Headquarters in Brussels represent their Chiefs of
Defence. Defence Ministries and Chiefs of Defence
maintain close contact with them.

'Allied Command Operations (ACO)' under the
Supreme Allied Commander Europe (SACEUR) at
Supreme Headquarters Allied Powers Europe (SHAPE)
in Mons, Belgium oversees NATO's military operations.

Sitting under ACO, Joint Force Command (JFC)
in Brunssum, Netherlands, was in 2005 broadly
speaking responsible for the defence of Northern and
Eastern Europe as its traditional NATO mission and for
ISAF in Afghanistan. JFC Naples was responsible
broadly speaking for the defence of Southern Europe
and for KFOR in Kosovo and the NATO training
mission in Iraq.

Other headquarters, mostly spread around
Europe, manage assets assigned to NATO. Ramstein,
Germany, where Allied Air Command is located, was
mentioned in the narrative.

Troop Contributing Nations (TCN) have
headquarters to manage all their military deployments
overseas. The UK Permanent Joint Headquarters at
Northwood was mentioned in the narrative. They give
instructions to their troops, receive regular reports, and
make visits to keep informed.

Allied Command Transformation (ACT)
located in Norfolk, Virginia, not shown on the diagram,
is at the same level in the structure as ACO/SHAPE and
oversees several entities. Mentioned in the narrative
were: Joint Warfare Centre, Stavanger, Norway and
Joint Analysis and Lessons Learned Centre, Lisbon,
Portugal.

NATO Officer Ranks 101

Four-Star General (Top of the tree in charge of a nation's Defences or a Service such as the Army or Air Force. Admiral in most Navies.)

Three-Star Lieutenant General (commands a 'Corps' of 100,000 or so troops.)

Two-Star Major General (commands a Division of 12-20,000 or so. UK's first General rank)

One-Star Brigadier General (Directs key functions in 3/4-Star led headquarters. Brigadier in UK can command a Brigade. Commodore in Royal Navy.)

Colonel (Can lead function in a big headquarters or command Brigade or equivalent, especially in US. Captain in Navies, Group Captain in some Air Forces, Oberst in Germany and Nordics.)

Lieutenant Colonel (Commands a unit/Battalion of 600-1200. Oberstleutnant Germany and Nordics. Commander in Royal Navy, as in Bond)

Major (Does the work in big headquarters. In UK commands Company of 100 or so. Squadron Leader in Royal Air Force.)

Captain (In most armies commands a Company (Dick Winters, 'Easy Company' Band of Brothers) Flight Lieutenant in RAF, commands 3-4 aircraft.)

Lieutenant (Platoon Commander or tank Troop Leader. Pilot Officer in RAF - flies aircraft.)

Second Lieutenant (Discontinued in UK. Sense of humour essential. Ensign, Midshipman.)

List of Maps

(Maps are the author's own)

11. An orientation map heads each week.

List of Images

(All images are the authors own. *Denotes embedded in orientation map for the week)

39. Bamiyan: scar left in rock after destruction of Buddha statue, pg101.
40. Bamiyan: High Street, Zuhak Antique & Handicraft, pg102.

Week Nine
41. Herat: Glass fronted offices and shops*, pg106.
42. Herat: apartment blocks/condo, pg111.

Week Ten
43. Salang Tunnel: North entrance*, pg113.
44. On route to Salang Tunnel: farmstead with tractor and abandoned armoured vehicle, pg115.
45. Dahani-i-Ghori: old man running shop, pg116
46. Dahani-i-Ghori: police post, pg117.
47. Dahani-i-Ghori: fighting partridge in wicker cage, pg119.
48. Dahani-i-Ghori: author in busy bazaar, pg119.
49. Dahani-i-Ghori: boys' school in UNHCR tents, pg120.
50. Dahani-i-Ghori: new clinic, pg121.

Week Eleven
51. Pol-e Khumri Bazaar: youths selling spices*, pg123.
52. CH-53G Stallion helicopter at Konduz, pg126.
53. Pol-e Khumri: tailor in bazaar with Singer sewing machines, pg127.

Week Twelve
54. Bagram: walled farms inter-connected to each other*, pg128.
55. Bagram: walled farm with orchards, pg131.

Week Thirteen
56. Burqa*, pg136.

Bibliography

Books, Poems, Lyrics.

Akiner, Shirin, *The Formation of Kazakh Identity, From Tribe to Nation-State*, 1995.

Allen, John R, and Felbab-Brown, Vanda, *The Fate of Women's Rights in Afghanistan*, 2020.

Amer, Ahmad Masood, *Afghanistan: The Journey of State Building and Democracy*, 2020.

Anon and George, Andrew, *The Epic of Gilgamesh,* 2003, Translation.

Armstrong, Karen, *Islam, A Short History*, 2002.

Aslan, Reza, *No God but God*, 2005.

Atwan, Abdel Bari, *After Bin Laden,* 2012.

Azoy, Witney G, *Buzkashi – Game and Power in Afghanistan,* 2003.

Babur and Thackston, W M, Trans, *Baburnama: Memoirs of Babur, Prince and Emperor*, 2002.

Bailey, Jonathan; Iron, Richard; and Strachan, Hew; Eds, *British Generals in Blair's Wars*, 2013.

Barry, Ben, *Blood, Metal and Dust: How Victory Turned into Defeat in Afghanistan and Iraq,* 2020.

Belousov, German, et al, *Afghanistan in Our Lives*, 1989.

Bobbitt, Phillip, *The Shield of Achilles: War, Peace, and the Course of History*, 2003.

Bogle, Eric, *Green Fields of France*, 1976.

Burns, Robert, *To A Mouse*, 1785.

Byron, Robert, *The Road to Oxiana*, 1937.

Dupree, Nancy Hatch, *An Historical Guide to Afghanistan,* 1977.

Elliott, Christopher L, *High Command, British Military Leadership in the Iraq and Afghanistan Wars*, 2017.

Engels, Fredrich, *The Conditions of the Working Class in England*, 1845.

Feifer, Gregory, *The Great Gamble, The Soviet War in Afghanistan*, 2009.

Fraser, George MacDonald, *Flashman*, 1969.

Gidardet, Edward; and Walter, Jonathan, *Afghanistan Essential Field Guide*, 2002.

Gray, John, *Al Qaeda and What it Means to be Modern*, 2003.

Griffin, Michael, *Reaping the Whirlwind, Afghanistan, Al Qa'ida and the Holy War*, 2003.

Heller, Joseph, *Catch-22,* 1961.

Hopkirk, Peter, *The Great Game,* 1990.

Hosseini, Khaled, *The Kite Runner*, 2003.

Kennedy, Charles Stuart, *Interview of Michael Metrinko for the Foreign Affairs Oral History Project*, 2005.

Lawrence, T E, *Seven Pillars of Wisdom*, 1926.

Ledwidge, Frank, *Losing Small Wars*, 2011.

Maclean, Fitzroy, *Eastern Approaches*, 1949.

Majrough, Sayd Bahodine, *Songs for Love and War, Afghan Women's Poetry,* 2010

Marquez, Gabriel Garcia, *One Hundred Years of Solitude*, 1967.

Marshall, Robert, *Storm from The East, from Genghis Khan to Khublai Khan,* 1994.

Newby, Eric, *A Short Walk in the Hindu Kush*, 1958.

Peach, L Du Garde, *Alexander the Great*, 1963.

Rashid, Ahmed, *Taliban,* 2001.

Sale, Lady Florentia, *A Journal of the Disasters in Afghanistan*, 1843.

Sakhwaraz, Bashir, *The Erotic and Revolutionary Poetry of Afghanistan*, PEN Transmissions, 2014.

Seierstad, Asne, *The Bookseller of Kabul*, 2003.

Stewart, Rory, *The Places In Between*, 2004.

Smith, Paul, *Princesses, Sufis, Dervishes, Martyrs & Feminists - Nine Great Women Poets of the East*, 2008.

Soufan, Ali, *Anatomy of Terror, From the Death of Bin Laden to the Rise of Islamic State*, 2017.

Tanner, Stephen, *Afghanistan: A Military History,* 2009.

Wheatcroft, Andrew, *The Ottomans,* 1995.

Movies, Series, and Video Clips.

633 Squadron, 1964, Walter Grauman.

Afghanistan-Woman Dies, Sep 2007, France 24.

Alien, 1979, Ridley Scott

Apocalypse Now, 1979, Francis Ford Coppola.

Band of Brothers, 2001, Tom Hanks.

Buzkashi Boys, 2011, Sam French

Charlie Wilson's War, 2008, Mike Nichols.

Commissar Amanullah, 2012, Sabah Sahar and Emal Zaki.

For a Few Dollars More, 1965, Sergio Leone.

Gallipoli, 1981, Peter Weir.

Game of Thrones, 2011-2019, David Benioff and D.B. Weiss.

Giving Birth in Afghanistan: Inside MSF's Baby Factory, 2018, MSF

Ice Cold in Alex, 1958, J Lee Thompson.

Kandahar, 2001, Mohsen Makhmalbaf.

Lord of the Rings, 2003, Peter Jackson.

Out of Africa, 1985, Sydney Pollack.

Reservoir Dogs, 1992, Quentin Tarantino.

Star Wars, 1977, and *The Empire Strikes Back*, 1980, George Lucas.

The Brigand of Kandahar, 1965, John Gilling.

The Horsemen, 1971, John Frankenheimer.

The Kite Runner, 2007, Marc Forster

The Man Who Would Be King, 1975, John Huston.

Thunderbirds, 1965, Gerry and Sylvia Anderson

Women in Love, 1969, Ken Russell.

Zorba the Greek, 1964, Michael Cacoyannis.

Zulu Dawn, 1979, Douglas Hickox.

Sites

www.afghanistan-analysts.org

www.archnet.org

www.britannica.com

www.cfr.org

www.en.wikipedia.org

www.gandhara.rferl.org

www.hrw.org

www.iln.org.uk

www.longwarjournal.org

www.nato.int

www.opendemocracy.net

www.pentransmissions.com

www.publicintelligence.net

www.SHAHMBOOKCO.com

www.watanchat.com

Abbreviations

ABP – Afghan Border Police.

AIHRC – Afghan Independent Human Rights Commission.

ANA – Afghan National Army.

ANP – Afghan National Police.

ANSF – Afghan National Security Forces.

ASNF – Afghan Special Narcotics Force.

ADF – Asia Development Fund.

ANSO – Afghan NGO Security Organization.

BCE – Before Common Era (BC in old speak).

CE – Common Era (AD in old speak).

CENTCOM – US Central Command.

CFC(A) – Combined Forces Command (Afghanistan).

CID – Criminal Investigation Department.

COMBRITFOR – Commander British Forces Afghanistan.

CPEF – Central Poppy Eradication Force.

CN – Counter Narcotics.

CNPA – Counter Narcotics Police of Afghanistan.

DDR – Disarm, Demobilize, Reintegrate.

DfID - Department for International Development.

DIAG – Disarming Illegal Armed Groups.

ESC – Executive Steering Committee.

ETTs – Embedded Training Teams.

EUPOL – European Union Police Mission.

FCO – Foreign and Commonwealth Office.

FSB – Forward Support Base.

GTZ – Gesellschaft fur Technische Zusammearbeit.

HALO - Hazardous Area Life-support Organization.

HMMWV (Humvee) – High Mobility Multi-purpose Wheeled Vehicle.

HRW – Human Rights Watch.
IOM – International Office for Migration.
ISAF – International Security Assistance Force.
ISI – Pakistan's Inter-Services Intelligence
JR – Judicial Reform.
LOTFA – Law and Order Trust Fund for Afghanistan.
LWJ – Long War Journal.
MoI – Ministry of Interior.
NAC – North Atlantic Council.
NATO – North Atlantic Treaty Organization.
NMC – NATO Military Committee.
NGO – Non-Government Organization.
NPP – National Priority Programmes.
MRRD – Ministry of Rural Reconstruction and Development.
PRT – Provincial Reconstruction Team.
R&R – Rest and Recuperation.
RCDS – Royal College of Defence Studies.
SACEUR – Supreme Allied Commander Europe.
SSR – Security Sector Reform.
UNDP – United Nations Development Programme.
UNAMA – United Nations Assistance Mission in Afghanistan.
UNESCO – United Nations Educational, Scientific and Cultural Organization.
UNHCR – United Nations High Commissioner for Refugees.
UNICEF – United Nations International Children's Emergency Fund.
UNODC – United Nations Office on Drugs and Crime.
UNOPS – United Nations Office for Project Services.
USAID – United States Agency for International Development.

Acknowledgements

I especially wish to thank my wife Dinah for holding the fort and for her laser beam editorial eye. Photographer daughter Mariette for advice on image selection. Son Sam for spotting the need for illustrated maps. Son Luke for early encouragement to 'put it out there'. My many dear friends, especially Nick Lipscombe for his inspiration and guidance; and Angus, Arthur, Nic, Phil, and Tony, for either being quick to say they would read it or providing wise counsel on content; and David for suggesting I liven it up by having an affair.

I acknowledge everyone I had the privilege of working with in Afghanistan whether in ISAF, the Coalition, Embassies, or Afghan Ministries and Security Forces. I am indebted for their friendship, support, insights and, in many cases, generous hospitality. I am especially grateful to Lieutenant General Erdagi for his wise leadership and for affording me so much scope.

Finally, my dear mother for imbuing in me from earliest childhood a life-enriching love of history.

About the Author

David Potts served as an officer in the British Army for thirty-seven years. He did stints in Germany, North America, Northern Ireland, Belize, Cyprus, and as a Brigadier in Kosovo, Afghanistan, Iraq, and East Africa. He then spent six years in London doing crisis management and corporate security in a global firm. Whilst serving in the Army he earned a bachelor's degree from Nottingham University and Carroll College Wisconsin, USA, and a master's degree from Kings College London. He attended the Royal College of Defence Studies. He was appointed a Member of the British Empire (MBE) by the UK and awarded a Legion of Merit Officer Class by the USA.

Printed in Great Britain
by Amazon

82785968R00159